WEST VALLEY COLLEGE LIBRARY

3 1216 00062 1

W9-BGY-091

WITHDRAWN

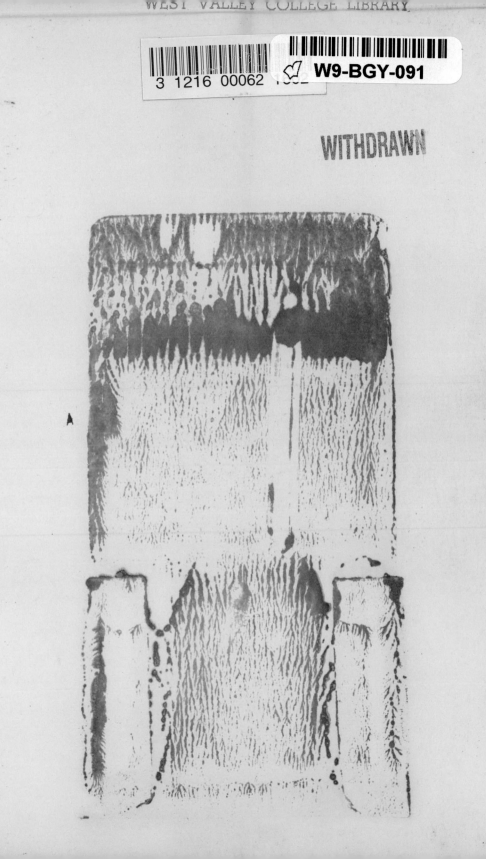

If Deer are to Survive

If Deer are to Survive

a Wildlife Management Institute book by
WILLIAM DASMANN

STACKPOLE BOOKS

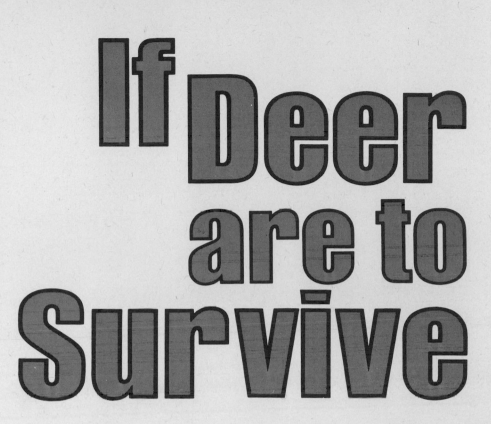

IF DEER ARE TO SURVIVE
Copyright © 1971 by
WILDLIFE MANAGEMENT INSTITUTE
Published by
STACKPOLE BOOKS
Cameron and Kelker Streets
Harrisburg, Pa. 17105

All rights reserved, including the right to reproduce this book or portions thereof in any form or by any means, electronic or mechanical, including photocopying, recording, or by any information storage and retrieval system, without permission in writing from the publisher. All inquiries should be addressed to Stackpole Books, Cameron and Kelker Streets, Harrisburg, Pennsylvania 17105.

Illustrations Courtesy

of the

Frederic C. Walcott Memorial Fund

of the

North American Wildlife Foundation

In the interests of conservation, this book is printed on 100% recycled paper.

ISBN 0-8117-0862-4
Library of Congress Catalog Card Number 79-162443

Printed in U.S.A.

32661

Contents

Acknowledgments 8

Foreword 9

Chapter 1 *The Evolution of Deer and Their Range* 11

How deer and their forage plants evolved together and the devastation that ensued when deer and livestock were introduced among plant communities not adapted to them

Chapter 2 *Elements of Deer Range* 13

Why the amount and location of food, water, and cover limit the population of deer herds and determine the size of their home ranges

Chapter 3 *Cover Requirements of Deer* 19

How logging or brush manipulation can be used to intermix cover and feeding areas and thus aid in maintaining and increasing deer populations

Chapter 4 *Water Needs of Deer* 25

When to supplement natural water supplies by bulldozing water holes and building check dams, sand traps, and rain catchments

Chapter 5 *Forage Relationships* 29

How recurring periods of scarcity result in constant reaction between the numbers of deer and the quantity and vitality of their forage plants

Chapter 6 *Food Preferences* 37

How evidence supplied by feeding penned deer, analyzing the contents of deer rumens, and examining browsed plants shows that deer choose forage for both its palatibility and digestibility

Chapter 7 *Nutritional Requirements of Deer* 45

How shortages of total food, protein, salt, minerals, and trace elements affect pregnancy rates, resistance to disease, weight, and antler development

Chapter 8 *Characteristics of Deer Forage* 56

How the proportion of grasses, forbs, and browse plants—for instance, sagebrush, bitterbrush, and oaks—in deer diets varies according to seasonal changes in the nutritional composition of each type of plant

Chapter 9 *Supplemental Feeding* 66

How artificial feeding, by encouraging the overbrowsing of deer-food plants and changing the diet of deer too abruptly, raises more problems than it solves under present conditions in North America

Chapter 10 *Herd Units and Seasonal Ranges* 70

How shortages on their most limited seasonal range limit the size of deer populations whether managed according to hunting area, biological unit, or land use zones

Chapter 11 *Predation and Competition* 74

Why predation by coyotes and bobcats fails to reduce deer numbers, and how livestock compete for food with deer more than naturalists formerly realized

Chapter 12 *Habitat Management in Brushlands* 81

How to manage habitat in brushlands to provide the species and growth stages of plants in patterns deer prefer by planting grass and browse, controlled burning, chemical brush control, and bulldozing browseways

Chapter 13 *Deer Habitat Management in Forests* 91

Why today's more efficient silviculture and the trend toward even-aged forests reduces deer habitat and necessitates closer cooperation between wildlife managers and foresters to maintain deer populations

Chapter 14 *Fundamentals of Deer Management* 102

Proper use of management tools and enlightened cropping of deer can alleviate the needless suffering and waste to benefit deer and man

Information Kit 108

Common and Scientific Names of Deer
Common and Scientific Names of Plants
Monthly Variation in Percentage of Crude Protein in Western Plants
Percentages of Crude Protein in Southern Browse Plants

References 114

Index 125

Acknowledgments

THE AUTHOR IS GREATLY INDEBTED TO MANY PEOPLE WHO ENCOURAGED and assisted in the completion and publication of this work. He is especially grateful to Everett E. Horn for his encouragement and direction toward publishing; to James B. Trefethen, for his constructive and patient editorial work; and to Everett Doman, A. E. Evanko, Walter O. Hanson, Richard L. Hubbard, Laurence R. Jahn, Louis A. Krumholz, Wallace G. Macgregor, Donald D. Strode, and Lonnie L. Williamson for their constructive reviews. He is grateful for offers of financial assistance from the California Wildlife Federation and the National Wildlife Federation and to the Wildlife Management Institute for bringing this work to fruition.

Foreword

OF ALL THE DIVERSE FORMS OF LARGE MAMMALS NATIVE TO NORTH America, the deer in their various species and races are the most abundant, most widely distributed, and—from the standpoint of recreation and economics—the most important group.

The past seventy years, which saw the development of the wildlife management movement, have demonstrated that deer are among the most adaptable and manageable of wild animals. They respond readily to habitat improvement and protective law. Where state wildlife agencies have full authority to manage the deer under sound biological principles, the herds can be regulated in size to maintain the proper balance between habitat and population that is essential to the health of the animals and the interests of farmers, foresters, and range managers.

The restoration of deer to their present abundance from the low point in the late 1800s, when the continental deer population could be counted in a few tens of thousands, is one of the crowning achievements of wildlife management. But it could not have been accomplished without the fortuitous circumstances that provided an abundance of ideal but unoccupied deer habitat at exactly the right time.

Brushlands and young forests that developed in the wake of widespread exploitative logging, farm abandonment, and protection from repeated forest fires in the early 1900s provided so much excellent habitat that deer managers could concentrate on protective law and restocking to restore the animals. We no longer can rely upon accident to produce the natural environment that is needed to support enough deer to satisfy mounting recreational and esthetic demands. Much of the deer habitat that was most productive a generation ago is declining sharply as the once-young forests mature and close out the sunlight essential for the growth of shrubs, herbs, and other plants that deer need for food.

We are entering an era in which more intensive management, especially habitat management, must be applied if the deer are to be maintained at anything near their present population levels. Nearly all existing deer range now is fully stocked and continues to deteriorate, and protection alone will not assure the survival of deer if this habitat continues to deteriorate as a result of natural plant succession.

Most woodland owners, farmers, foresters, ranchers, and range managers enjoy having deer around. In some areas deer hunting privileges are a major source of supplementary income to private landowners. Everywhere deer hunting is an important form of recreation to millions of outdoorsmen. Cooperative programs between wildlife managers, foresters, and range managers on state and national forests and some private lands show that deer can be maintained with little or no conflict with the primary economic use of an area, whether it be the production of pulpwood, timber, or beef. Years of thoughtful wildlife research have provided the know-how to do much more. All that is required is the application of known practices to the land. In many instances these represent only modifications of existing range or forest cultural practices, many of which benefit other resources than deer. Water holes and open strips, for example, have obvious values in fire suppression.

The Wildlife Management Institute, in publishing this book, believes that it will contribute to the public understanding of deer management opportunities and that, in addition to wildlife students and technicians, it will be especially useful to foresters, range managers, and other land managers who are interested in maintaining or increasing the deer herds on the lands under their control.

DANIEL A. POOLE
President, Wildlife Management Institute

CHAPTER 1

The Evolution of Deer and Their Range

DEER HAVE OCCUPIED THE NORTH AMERICAN CONTINENT FOR MANY millions of years. The species we know today have existed essentially in their present forms for about a million years. During this long period of time the deer and the environment evolved together. Each was honed by the slow but immutable processes of natural selection into fine adjustment with the other.

Species of plants that were not able to withstand the impact of deer browsing disappeared long ago from the deer range. Gone, too, are those forms of the deer family that could not accommodate to changes in the environment.

This is not to say that deer populations in prehistoric times were not subject to fluctuations like those that occur today. During favorable periods deer, no doubt, multiplied to population levels that led to overbrowsing and depletion of range and the physical degradation and death of animals from disease and malnutrition. But in nature's slow schedule such setbacks matter little. A recovery lasting fifty, five hundred, or a thousand years occupies only a second on the earth's geological time clock. Maladjustments of this kind undoubtedly occurred with relative frequency. In the main, however, animals and the environment got along together.

An environmental balance of this kind does not always occur where animals and their range have not had the benefit of close evolutionary relationship. We have only to turn to New Zealand for an example.

The red deer of Europe was introduced in 1851 to an island where the native plant communities had developed without browsing by ruminants. The red deer not only prospered, it multiplied beyond relief. Today it is classified as a pest. Although many of the native plants of New Zealand were palatable and nutritious, they had not been prepared by evolution to withstand heavy browsing. A host of plant species were depleted soon after the introduction of deer. Some have nearly disappeared from extensive areas (91)*.

We can find a similar example much closer to home. The pioneer's cows and sheep were turned out in high numbers on North American ranges that had withstood the Pleistocene horse and camel, and later, the bison, elk, pronghorn, and deer. But the ranges had not been conditioned by evolution to withstand the repeated close grazing and browsing of domestic livestock. The result was a startling depletion of vegetation, often followed by serious loss of soil. In some parts of the West, original range vegetation exists now only as remnant stands and patches in places that have offered it natural protection. Vast areas have been taken over by more aggressive and hardier plants, many of which were introduced from lands with a long history of livestock grazing (34).

In the long span of time, it matters little whether a deer population damages its ranges and goes into a prolonged decline. But it does matter to man today. Society has an interest in maintaining optimum-sized populations of game animals for sport, for esthetic enjoyment, and for scientific reasons. This has led man to investigate the life histories and environmental needs of the wild animals with which he shares this planet.

The following chapters will present some of the facts we know about the needs of deer. They will tell how deer range must be managed to maintain deer herds in relatively stable numbers, in balance with their habitat, and with other uses of the land.

---

* Numbers in parentheses refer to numbered references in the back of this book.

CHAPTER 2

Elements of Deer Range

THE QUALITY OF DEER RANGE IS AFFECTED BY MANY VARIABLE FACTORS other than the activities of man. There is topography—the lay of the land—north slope, south slope, high mountain or low valley. There are soil conditions, natural water supplies, and plants. There are other animals. All of these are affected by climate and weather, and sometimes and in some places, by wildfire. Some of these factors foster, some suppress, and some appear to have no influence at all on the survival of deer.

We might picture the elements necessary for deer survival as a triangle, the points of which are food, water, and cover (118). Not all vegetation is deer food. Some plants that deer do eat are good foods; others are poor. Water may occur free—in ponds, streams, or springs; or it may be present less conspicuously as moisture in fresh, green grass or leaves. Cover may be classified by its use—shade, shelter, camouflage, and escape.

Adequate food, good water, and cover in a suitable arrangement are essential to the survival of deer. This is as true in the broad sense of the range of a deer herd as it is, in the narrow sense, for an indi-

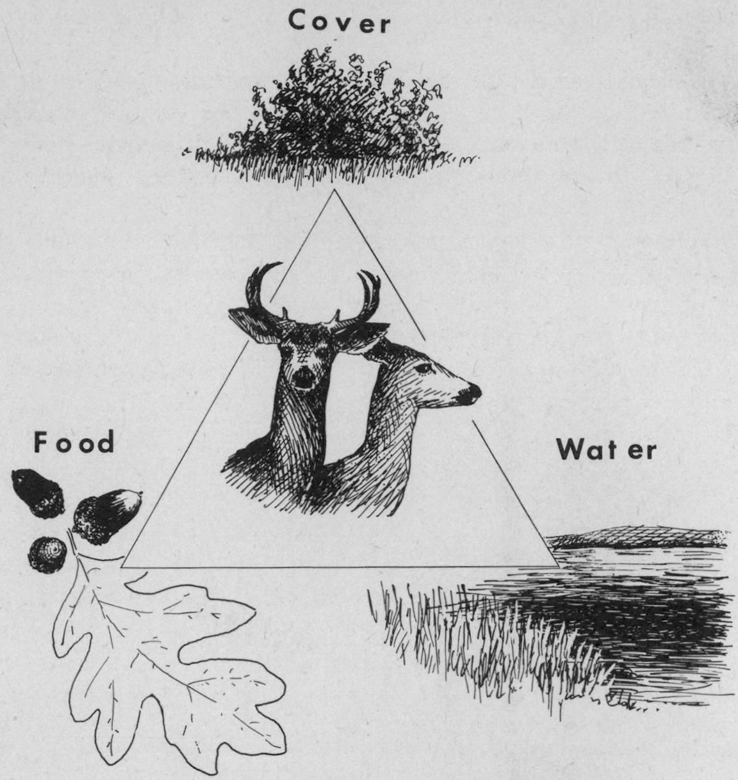

Elements Necessary for Deer Survival

Adequate and properly distributed food, water, and cover are essential ingredients of deer range.

vidual deer or a family group. When all elements are present in proper balance and relationship, deer appear able to cope with factors that tend to suppress their survival.

Where food, cover, and water are close together, the range of a family group may be small. Home ranges of nonmigratory black-tailed doe-yearling-fawn groups in northern coastal California average less than a half-mile in diameter, those of bucks about three-fourths of a mile (169).

Migratory deer may travel as much as 100 miles between summer and winter ranges. But the individual bucks and family groups of does, fawns, and yearlings usually live within limited areas on each seasonal range to which they tend to return year after year. Individual winter ranges of California mule deer in the Sierra Nevada average less than one-half mile in diameter and summer ranges between one-half and three-fourths of a mile (118). Rocky Mountain mule deer in Montana,

Oregon, Nevada, and Utah behave no differently. Studies in all these states show that the deer use little more on the average than half a square mile of winter range and one square mile of summer range (74, 145, 182). In the spruce-fir forests of Montana, the summer home ranges of deer seldom exceed 100 acres (179).

Desert mule deer in the arid brush country of Arizona have home ranges from one to two and a half miles in diameter (165). Here the points of the food-water-cover triangle are more widely spaced.

The use of limited individual territory is not a trait confined to mule deer. On the Edwards Plateau in Texas, white-tailed deer trapped and tagged in a number of different studies were seldom found more than a mile and a half from the sites where they were first marked. The average distance was four-tenths of a mile (79, 173).

In Wisconsin 91 percent of whitetails tagged on winter range were recovered by hunters in November within 7.5 miles of the trapping site. The average distance was 3.5 miles (28). White-tailed deer in Wisconsin are not migratory, but large numbers summer on areas some distance from their limited winter yarding areas. The year-long range of each individual probably includes separate and relatively small tracts of summer and winter range and the travel routes between.

Whitetails probably use the same winter range year after year. Four of twenty-five deer trapped in Wisconsin in a winter yard had been tagged on the same site three years earlier, one two years earlier, and four in the previous year (28). Reports from Michigan and Minnesota indicate similar behavior in those states (6, 134).

Although mule deer may migrate 100 miles between summer and winter ranges, the areas of these individual ranges are surprisingly small.—*Photo by W. G. Macgregor, California Department of Fish and Game*

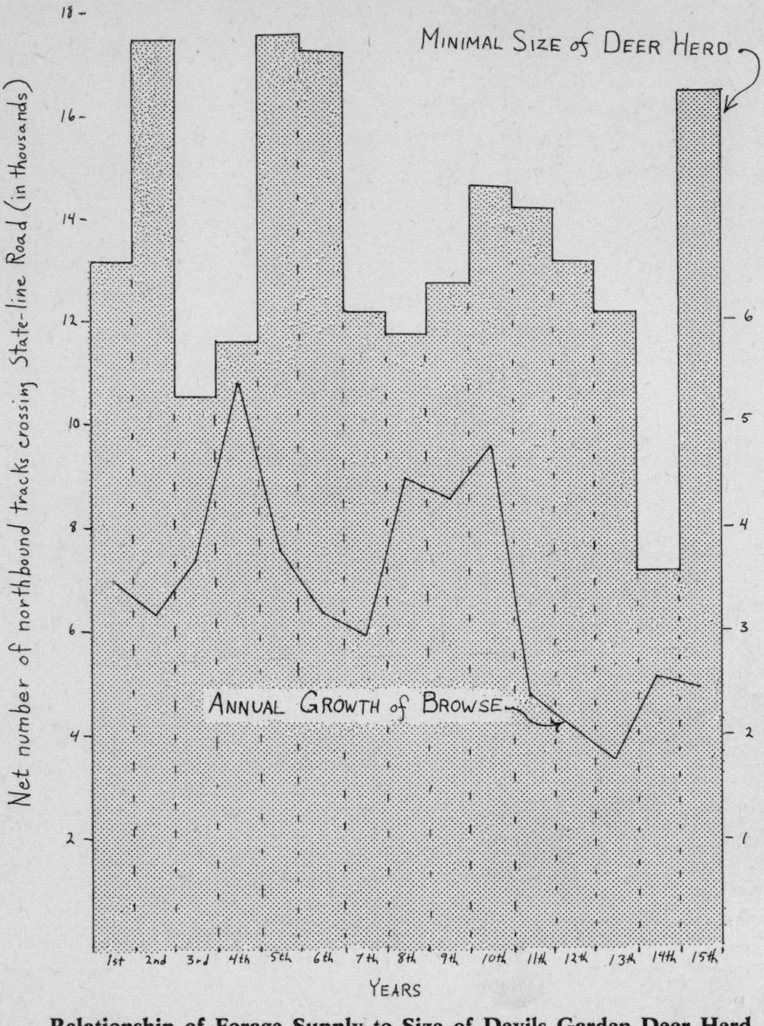

Relationship of Forage Supply to Size of Devils Garden Deer Herd

The graph shows fluctuations in a deer population that has reached a level close to the maximum carrying capacity of its range, based on annual track counts over 16 years, and the relationship of the annual forage supply.—*Compiled from data in the reports of the Devils Garden Interstate Deer Committee, 1949-1965*

Home ranges of deer must offer food, water, and cover, It follows that any changes in the range that create more or closer combinations of these three elements will tend to increase deer numbers.

The level of population at which a deer herd is most productive is called the optimum density. This is the population level at which all the animals have adequate food, water, and cover but above which one or more of these vital elements runs into short supply (41).

Unmanaged deer herds usually increase beyond optimum density to the maximum carrying capacity of their habitat. When this happens, the population maintains a rough balance with a fluctuating food supply. Occasionally the water supply, and less frequently the available cover, may be the limiting factor. At the maximum level, one deer must die to make room for another, and most of the animals suffer from seasonal shortages. The number of deer that survive in any one year under such conditions is the most the range will support during the season of shortest supply (see the accompanying graph). The surplus animals die. Sometimes the losses are evident and spectacular, as they are during concentrated winter die-offs. Or they may go relatively unnoticed and unseen as they usually are among deer that die from day to day over an extensive area.

Whitetails probably use the same winter range year after year.—*Photo courtesy Ontario Department of Lands and Forests*

The amount of available food, cover, and water places a ceiling on the deer population of a range. The size of a range may also limit the number of deer it can support. Not much has been reported about the spatial requirements of wild deer. Aldo Leopold concluded that there was little visible evidence of any density limit in hoofed animals except the carrying capacity of the food supply (115). He pointed out that nowhere in the wild do densities approach those the animals tolerate in confinement.

More recent studies, however, indicate that spatial limits do exist, at least among deer. On a chaparral brush range in north coastal California, the saturation level for breeding blacktail does appears to be about thirty-six to the square mile, or one to eighteen acres (169). Although spatial requirements may vary with differing food-water-cover combinations, there is little doubt that there is a limit beyond which crowding becomes detrimental.

This results not only from intensified competition for food, water, and cover and the increased possibility of spreading disease and parasites but also from tensions caused by social stress. Up to this limit, however, range carrying capacity can be increased through balanced habitat improvements. These may include cover manipulation, development or improvement of water supplies, or increase in quantity and quality of food.

CHAPTER 3

Cover Requirements of Deer

COVER CONTRIBUTES TO THE WELL-BEING OF DEER BY PROVIDING shelter from the elements, by increasing their chances of escape from enemies, and by fostering a sense of security. A number of recent studies, in fact, indicate that the security factor may be important in maintaining deer in good physical condition.

The nature of acceptable cover—whether dense or open, tall or short—and distances the animals will venture from it (the security zone) vary with the nature and severity of the hazards common to the site. In one place or another cover must alleviate to tolerable limits the cold, wetness, and snow depths of winter; the heat and insect annoyance of summer; and harassment by predators and hunters.

Although we usually think of deer cover as consisting of trees and shrubs, it can be provided as well in some areas by topographical features—scattered boulders, lava breaks, marsh vegetation, gullies and draws, or the lee sides of ridges.

Deer must eat and drink to survive, but their needs for cover tend to vary with local or regional conditions. When the climate is mild and enemies few, deer can thrive in minimal cover. But as heat or cold

Cover, among other values, fosters a sense of security in deer.—*Photo by Bill Cross, Maine Fish and Game Department*

intensifies, snow depths mount, or predators and hunters increase, deer's need for cover becomes more critical.

Deer use cover more in some seasons of the year and some periods of the day than in others. In south coastal California, black-tailed deer try to avoid direct sunlight on hot summer days. As sunlight and shadows shift, they change their bedding locations to remain in the shade (120). Both whitetails and blacktails will move day and night to avoid high or low temperatures. In north coastal California, the deer seem to prefer an air temperature between 55° and 65°F. (169).

Most livestock owners know the importance to cattle of shade from the hot summer sun. Cows or steers cannot maintain normal body temperatures when subjected to air temperatures above 80°F. Full-fed steers on range with adequate shade gain up to 40 percent more weight than those on shadeless pasture (65).

At the other end of the scale, escape from the chilling blasts of winter seems more important to deer than a supply of food (81). During periods of intense cold, especially when they are accompanied by high winds, deer seek shelter in coniferous or other heavy cover, usually on the lee sides of ridges (153). They will search out and remain in such areas during severe weather even if food is lacking.

Studies in Pennsylvania show that whitetails increase in weight when supplied average to good-quality food, so long as the temperature remains above 40°F. When the thermometer falls below that level, the deer begin to lose weight. When the mercury falls below 30°, they lose weight rapidly no matter how nutritious their food supply or how much they eat (66). There is little doubt that deer lose less body heat during severe winter weather on ranges with adequate cover. Thus the presence of good cover on winter range may allow them to survive at a lower plane of nutrition than that required where cover is inadequate.

In northern Maine, where snows are deep and winter climates severe, food and winter cover must be separated by distances no greater than 100 yards to be useful to deer (69). California black-tailed deer seldom feed in openings more than 100 yards from cover (169). It is unusual, in fact, to find deer much more than 400 yards from cover of some sort.

These facts and the food-water-cover triangle should be remembered in planning habitat improvements for deer. The creation of one or more new triangles by cover development will elevate the overall carrying capacity of an area, but it will not necessarily increase the

White-tailed deer in northern Maine select nearly pure stands of mature conifers as winter yarding areas. This yard has been improved by judicious logging, which permits the development of essential browse.—*Photo courtesy Maine Department of Inland Fisheries and Game*

capacity of those triangles that already exist. Planting patches of cover on open ranges supporting deer forage plants, for example, may benefit animals whose home ranges overlap or are immediately adjacent to the new cover. These deer may extend their territories into the new range or eventually shift into it. But the improvements may provide no benefit at all to deer with home-range boundaries only a half-mile distant (169).

White-tailed deer in northern Maine select nearly pure stands of mature conifers with all but closed canopies as winter yarding areas. The amount of forage on adjacent areas determines the number of deer the yard will support. In that part of the country a pattern of long, narrow strips of mature pine, spruce, or other conifers separated by lanes of open bushy cover about 100 yards wide approaches the ideal winter range for deer. Timber operators can encourage deer and other wildlife by leaving uncut strips of heavy coniferous cover along stream courses and around pond and lake margins. The adjacent cutover lands with their regenerating herbaceous and shrubby vegetation provide feeding areas (69). Several paper and lumber companies with large holdings in northern New England arrange their cutting operations to provide such cover in cooperation with state wildlife agencies.

Both the need for dense cover and the distance between cover and food become less critical as we move southward. In southern Maine, for instance, deer find acceptable winter shelter in open mixed stands of hardwoods and conifers and range farther from cover in search of food (69).

Where the climate is even more temperate, the proportion of the winter range that must be devoted to cover decreases and that which may be managed for food production expands.

A similar relationship among deer, cover, and climate probably exists in the West. Black-tailed deer yard in cedar swamps or thickets of second-growth timber when snow in the open country becomes deep (26). On parts of Vancouver Island, British Columbia, the only known limiting factor for deer is the absence of standing timber to provide shelter when winter comes (147). On the Jawbone winter range in California, pine timber stands are preferred bedding grounds for mule deer in inclement weather (118). In the same state, on the Pilot Ridge winter range on the west slope of the Sierra Nevada, deer winter under live oak trees when snow depths in open areas reach eighteen inches. Under the trees, depths average only eight inches (50).

Those who know deer realize that there can be such a thing as too much cover as well as too little. On millions of acres the problem is to open up existing cover rather than to plant more of it. A patchwork pattern of interspersed vegetation types is far more favorable to deer than extensive solid stands of brush or even-aged timber. Deer, like many other species of wildlife, prefer the edges of vegetation types —the borders of forests where they merge into cutover lands, the shrubby cover between woodland and meadow, and the margins of brushlands adjacent to openings.

Cover development, therefore, may consist of introducing vegetation of a suitable type into areas where there is little or none, or it may involve opening extensive stands of dense brush or timber to intermix cover and feeding areas. Planting cover on an area where woody vegetation is in short supply can extend deer range, providing it is near food and water. Creating openings in dense cover can increase the number of deer on an existing range.

There are innumerable examples from all over North America to indicate the usefulness of the latter method. A seven-year study of black-tailed deer on chaparral range in California showed that both deer numbers and fawn production and survival could be increased by cover manipulation. Throughout this study, unmanaged brush range carried a stable population of 20 deer per square mile. On the managed part of the range, where the cover was converted to open stands of shrubs mixed with herbaceous vegetation, the deer population rose to 50 and 60 per square mile (11).

If dense brush limits deer numbers, the effect of heavy timber is even more pronounced. In spite of a common impression, white-tailed deer were not abundant in eastern Canada, northern New England, and in much of the forested region around the Great Lakes when the first settlers reached America. Dense coniferous forests with few openings and little deer food could not support many whitetails.

It was only after the settler and homesteader with their axes and fires opened the forest that deer became abundant. In the eastern United States white-tailed deer probably were most numerous in precolonial times around Indian towns, in burned areas, and in the prairie fringes of the eastern forest from Minnesota southward. In Saskatchewan today, deer are most numerous in the parklands where prairie grasses and forest trees merge. Nearby dense forests support only from three to six deer per square mile (168).

The mature Douglas fir forests of western Washington carry no more than ten black-tailed deer to each square mile. Twenty years after the stands are logged, the deer population often increases to sixty per square mile. After the twenty-year peak, the population begins to decline rapidly as the regenerating forest starts to shade out the ground cover. Thirty-five years after cutting, it drops to around ten

The need for dense cover is less critical in the South than in the North.—*Photo courtesy U.S. Forest Service*

per square mile. At the end of fifty-five years, when the young trees attain full density, the population falls to four or five per square mile (14).

A similar situation prevails in the redwood region of northwestern California. A typical square mile of virgin redwood and mixed coniferous forest supports only about two blacktails. Five years after the timber is cut, the deer population increases sevenfold. The increase is twentyfold at the end of ten years. Then a decline begins. Twenty years after logging, the population is not significantly higher than it was before the cutting (31).

Ordinarily deer will not deplete their own cover except where the important cover plants also are used for food. In such situations, the animals may open up the cover through their browsing. Usually this results in well-defined "browse lines" on the older, taller shrubs and trees and hedging on the younger, shorter plants.

In some areas, it is far more practical to regulate deer numbers to the optimum carrying capacity of existing ranges than to engage in costly cover development. But in many areas, there is need to improve cover patterns, either directly or as a side benefit of multipurpose brush-to-grass type conversion, timber-cutting, or reforestation.

CHAPTER 4

Water Needs of Deer

SOME KINDS OF ANIMALS CAN MANUFACTURE THEIR OWN WATER FROM the foods they eat and need never take a drink. Despite some barbershop tales, deer do not belong in this category. Deer must have water. An adequate water supply is an essential ingredient of all deer ranges.

But the need of deer for water is much less during periods when succulent vegetation is abundantly available than when the plants are dry or dormant. Air temperature, evaporation rates, water content of the prevailing food, and extent of exercise all influence the amount of water a deer drinks each day (133).

A number of studies of captive deer have been made in different areas to determine their water requirements under varying conditions. In southern Arizona, the average daily consumption of water is between one and one and a half quarts per animal hundredweight in winter and from two to three quarts in summer (133). In New York State, captive white-tailed deer on artificial food and with access to a salt lick drank an average of three quarts per hundredweight daily in winter (124).

An adequate supply of water is an essential ingredient of deer range.—*Photo courtesy U.S. Forest Service*

Eastern deer use very little open water when snow is present. Captive deer on a diet of alfalfa hay and browse in the New York study appeared satisfied where no water other than snow was available (124). Research workers in Massachusetts tracked whitetails in winter and found that they made no attempt to use open water in sixty-one miles of travel (93). Because deer have water requirements similar to those of other ruminants, however, prolonged snowless periods of intense cold may cause trouble by locking all of the normally available drinking water in ice.

Water undoubtedly may be the limiting factor for deer populations in arid areas. It is self-evident, too, that prolonged drought may decrease the number of deer in more or less direct ratio to the decline of free water on their ranges. Even on the more arid ranges, however, there is usually more water available than is apparent to the casual observer. Intensive studies usually reveal the presence of water sources in the forms of seeps, pools, and small springs (169).

The quality of the local water supply may be as important to deer as quantity. In Arizona, there appears to be a close connection between fawn mortality and the amount and condition of the available water. On several ranges a direct association was found between a high fawn mortality and a low, stagnant water supply (133). In California, a deficient water supply, coupled with poor range conditions, was suspected by research workers of being a major contributing factor in an outbreak of foot rot, or necrobacillosis. Concentrations of deer using muddy areas around water holes apparently favor spread of this disease. The only practical controls known at this time are intensified range management and development of new watering areas to break up the concentrations of deer (149).

The water supply of an area usually is governed by climate, but it can be affected by soil type, geologic structure, range condition, density of vegetation, and fire.

When the plant cover on a range is depleted or destroyed by overgrazing, uncontrolled fire, or prolonged drought, rain falls directly on the bare, unprotected soil. Root channels and soil pores become plugged with silt; sparse surviving plants are unable to retain or deflect the rivulets. As a consequence, water tends to run off at once instead of sinking into the ground to become available later in the form of seeps and springs (38).

Dense stands of willows, alders, and other water-loving plants along the banks of small creeks or around springs sometimes absorb and transpire so much water as to reduce or even dry up the source. This problem is most prevalent and most critical in water-deficient areas, but it can occur during periods of drought in the more humid regions.

The influence of fire on water supplies is still a debatable subject.

Additional supplies of water can increase the carrying capacity for deer in arid areas. This water hole on the Mendecino National Forest in California was created to impound the waters from a seep.—*Photo courtesy U.S. Forest Service*

Undoubtedly fire affects each local situation differently. Where controlled burning is used successfully to replace woody vegetation with grass, the result may be a net gain in water production. Burning riparian vegetation and dense growth around springs and seeps also may increase water flows. On the other hand, fire so intense as to denude the land may produce accelerated runoff on some soils and reduce the year-long water supply.

Where water supplies are deficient or unreliable, the provision of additional watering places for deer may be an essential range improvement. Optimum spacing appears to be about one-half mile. Development may involve only clearing and boxing a spring or constructing a trough to concentrate and hold an otherwise dispersed water supply. Small reservoirs and water holes blasted or bulldozed in the national and state forests of the Appalachians, primarily for forest fire suppression, are heavily used by whitetails. Other methods are more costly. Check dams or sand traps in the beds of intermittent streams or washes will often retain enough water to maintain deer between rains. Small paved rain catchments leading to underground reservoirs and thence to troughs have been widely used in the Southwest.

Water development for deer usually is expensive, especially in areas where it is needed most. It can be justified only where a clear-cut shortage exists, and costs must be weighed carefully against the expected economic and esthetic returns. There are situations in many arid areas, however, where water development, adequately planned and properly spaced, may be the key to a larger deer population.

Water catchment devices like this can open up extensive areas of arid brushland to deer use.—*Photo courtesy U.S. Forest Service*

CHAPTER 5

Forage Relationships

FOOD IS USUALLY THE WEAKEST POINT IN THE FOOD-WATER-COVER triangle. This is because deer feed almost exclusively on plants, which must be spared a portion of their growth if they are to survive.

Deer generally cannot damage their water supplies, and only rarely do they destroy their cover. But through heavy browsing, they can deplete their food supplies.

Heavy cropping of leaves and twigs by feeding deer can reduce the activity of a plant to a level at which it is unable to sustain normal growth. As the plant approaches this level, twigs and branches begin to die and the root system to shrivel. Unable to process sufficient foods because of the loss of foliage, it goes into decline. Viable seed production is reduced or stops entirely. If the heavy browsing continues long enough, the result is decadence and finally death of the plant.

THE FORAGE MAINTENANCE RESERVE

That part of the annual growth of plants that can be removed without causing loss of vigor is commonly called the *allowable forage crop* (98).

That portion that must be left to maintain the plant and to protect the soil may be called the *forage maintenance reserve* (37).

Deer need an adequate supply of nutritious forage. The amount of food that will be produced each year, under given growing conditions, depends upon the maintenance reserve. A deer manager must be as much concerned with the amount of herbage left at the end of the growing season as with that consumed by range animals (98).

ALLOWABLE USE FACTOR

The level of use of its annual growth that a plant can sustain without damage is called the *allowable use factor.* Considerable work has been done to determine the allowable use factors of different species of plants, but these studies have largely been confined to grasses. Perennial grasses vary by species in the amount of leafage that can be safely grazed. This ranges from 45 percent by weight for such species as Idaho fescue to 60 percent for June grass. Desert salt grass can be

Some types of shrubbery vegetation can provide good deer habitat over long periods of time because their density and composition are relatively stable.—*Photo by William L. Van Allen*

grazed to a one-inch stubble, while bluebunch wheatgrass suffers if grazed below the five-inch level (121).

Much less effort has been spent to determine the browsing tolerance of shrubs and trees, the primary foods of deer. Moreover, the work that has been reported is confused somewhat by varying objectives of the investigators. Some have sought to measure the extent to which plants (particularly trees) can be browsed without retarding height growth; others have concerned themselves with productivity of forage. The browsing tolerance of red maple, for example, was assigned by one forestry-oriented investigator at 20 percent utilization (150); yet red maple is known to persist in spite of much heavier browsing (139).

Enough work has been done, however, to indicate that allowable use factors for most deer browse plants fall between 40 and 65 percent (Table 1). The level of browsing that results in closely cropped and

TABLE 1

ALLOWABLE USE FACTORS FOR BROWSE SPECIES

Species	Percent Utilization	Reference
	Western Species	
Aspen	65-70	(103)
Bitterbrush	50-65	(86)
Cliff rose	50-65	(103)
Honeysuckle	60-65	(181)
Serviceberry	60-65	(86)
Wild lilac	50-60	(181)
Wild rose	60-65	(86)
Snowbrush	35-40	(86)
Redstem	60	(86)
	Eastern Species	
Blackberry	30-40	(150)
Dog hobble	10	(150)
Greenbrier	50-60	(150, 152)
Beauty-berry	40	(80)
Flowering dogwood	50	(80)
Northern white cedar	25	(3)
Red bay	40	(80)
Red maple (North)	40	(80)
Red maple (South)	20	(80)
Smooth hydrangea	40	(80)
Sourwood	40	(80)
Tulip poplar	30	(150)
Yaupon	40	(80)
Yellow jessamine	50	(80)

tightly hedged shrubs may be considered excessive for most plants, but not all, such as mountain maple (107).

A plant's resistance to browsing may vary with season or site. In Idaho, 50 percent use of the new growth on wild lilac in early summer may be excessive; but wild lilac can withstand up to 60 percent browsing in late summer and fall (181). Greenbrier in the upland oak-chestnut forests of North Carolina can maintain itself under 60 percent utilization; that in hardwood coves should receive no more than 50 percent use (152). Heavy browsing causes the least damage during the winter dormant season, because at that time the food reserves of most plants are concentrated in the root system.

The amount of browse that can be cropped from a tree without affecting its future output varies with its height. On northern white cedars over ten feet tall, browsing of the lower branches merely hastens the death of limbs that would be lost to normal self-pruning. On those up to ten feet tall, however, more of the foliage is within reach of the deer; such trees cannot maintain an output of browse if more than 25 percent of this foliage is removed (3).

Allowable use factors are meant to apply to individual plants. The average use of a stand of plants of any one species may need to be less than the allowable use factor for individual plants of that species. This is because animals do not forage uniformly over a range. On the Devils Garden winter range of California, for example, about 40 percent of the bitterbrush plants were browsed too heavily, although the average use of the stand was only 41 percent (100). This is too much to sacrifice. On the other hand, if the same intensity of browsing had been distributed evenly over the entire range, an average of 41 percent could be satisfactory.

Allowable use factors for various browse species help us evaluate various levels of stocking by range animals. In the final analysis, however, the stocking level, either for deer or livestock, must be governed by its effect on the overall range.

ANIMAL UNITS

Stocking rates for western livestock ranges usually are expressed in terms of animal units. An animal unit is defined as a 1,000-pound cow or its equivalent in horses, sheep, or other plant-eating animals. On the basis of studies at Utah State College, a 1,000-pound range cow will eat 15 to 27 pounds of hay each day; a 125-pound range ewe in winter requires from 3 to 3.8 pounds of food daily (135). A host of studies show that deer need from 2.4 to 2.8 pounds of air-dry forage each day per hundredweight, or from 5 to 7 pounds of green browse (67, 133, 166, 171).

The amount of forage required by a ruminant is related more to the area of its heat-radiating surface than directly to its size or weight. Air-dry forage requirements, however, have been found to be proportional to the seventy-three hundredth power of the live weight of the animal (12). Applying this formula to deer of different weights we find the following requirements (18):

100-pound deer	2.80 pounds air-dry forage a day
150-pound deer	3.88 pounds air-dry forage a day
200-pound deer	4.78 pounds air-dry forage a day
250-pound deer	5.63 pounds air-dry forage a day
300-pound deer	6.43 pounds air-dry forage a day

This indicates that a 150-pound deer will eat as much food as a range ewe, or about one-fifth as much as a 1,000-pound range cow.

This would suggest that five 150-pound deer would be equal to one animal unit. But direct conversion of livestock units to deer units may lead to error (105, 144). Diets and food preferences of deer and livestock vary considerably from place to place and may not always overlap, especially on range where forage is plentiful. Utah investigators estimate that it may be necessary to remove as many as 32 deer to make room for one additional cow or four cows to provide forage for five more deer (164). In Texas, it was estimated that 15 to 20 deer on properly stocked range eat no more grass than a single range cow. The Texans, however, found that deer consume much greater quantities of grass when browse is short in supply (45).

CARRYING CAPACITY

We have referred to carrying capacity several times. Its meaning is more or less self-evident. The term is used so often with loose definition, however, that it seems advisable to qualify it with adjectives.

We shall use *maximum carrying capacity* to denote the greatest number of animals that the range will carry on a strictly maintenance basis. Nothing in nature is static, including the maximum carrying capacity of a deer range. The population ceiling of a unit will rise during favorable years and fall during poor years. Many die-offs of deer result from such fluctuations. The herd will increase during a succession of favorable years to a population level much higher than the normal ceiling, only to face severe readjustment when changing conditions result in a rapid drop in carrying capacity. During such adjustment periods, severe range damage may, and often does, occur.

In forests, and in some chaparral brush types, deer forage often becomes abundant after logging, fire, or other disturbance. But this abundance may be relatively short-lived as the returning cover matures. The forage grows out of reach or becomes too coarse or dense to provide much deer food. The carrying capacity will soon decline no matter what the level of deer numbers. From the standpoint of the range, it may not matter whether the deer increase to maximum capacity on such areas (33). But from the animals' standpoint it does matter since shortages of one kind or another will occur prematurely, reduce herd productivity, and cause a decline in the condition and health of the deer.

Some types of shrubby vegetation can provide good deer habitat over long periods of time because their density and composition are relatively stable. Stocking of such areas at maximum levels will damage the range and result in fluctuating deer populations.

Because the maximum carrying capacity varies from year to year in response to weather conditions, a line graph illustrating annual deer numbers under maximum stocking usually resembles a profile chart of mountainous terrain, with high peaks in years of plenty falling off into deep population troughs in years of want.

Management plans for deer should aim at holding numbers below the maximum level at the optimum carrying capacity (41). The *optimum carrying capacity* is the number of animals a range will carry in good condition on a sustained basis; that is, without damage or depletion of an essential element of the range. It is a relatively stable number of animals, the demands of which permit maintenance of soil productivity and a cover of desirable forage plants.

OVERBROWSING

Species of palatable forage plants that were unable to withstand browsing disappeared from the deer ranges ages ago. Those that occur today survive because they were able to withstand the losses inflicted on them by deer. Most have a high tolerance to heavy pruning, attain rapid height growth, develop thorny cagelike branch patterns that protect their interior foliage, or have other adaptations that assure their survival. By one means or another, enough of these native plants have been able to withstand periodic ravages of large numbers of deer to perpetuate themselves over broad areas, even though locally many of them may be damaged.

Overpopulation leads to overbrowsing, and overbrowsing lowers the carrying capacity of the range. This overbrowsed yard will not support many deer next winter.—*Photo courtesy Maine Fish and Game Department*

When deer become too plentiful for the food supply on their range, the damage that occurs becomes a two-edged sword that cuts into both range and deer. When deer become so numerous that they must use the range maintenance reserve, the kinds of plants that they like best are the first to suffer. Many of these plants fall into a class called *critical deer forages*. These are foods that are vital to the well-being of the animals. Some may provide a sustaining diet during times when most vegetation is inadequate for this purpose. Or they may help the deer maintain body fat far enough into an adverse period to permit the animals to survive until conditions improve (41, 147).

A reduction in the supply of critical forage will lower the carrying capacity of the range. Such food shortages cause a decline in the physical condition of deer and lower their resistance to disease and parasites. Inadequately fed deer also are more prone to death by accident and predation. Inevitably food shortages cause loss of weight, size, and vigor and lower the rate of productivity, serving as natural checks on further population growth.

Moreover, heavy browsing results in a decline in plant vigor and lowers the forage production. This cuts the available food supply still further and edges the herd closer to the brink of disaster. At this point, a drought, a severe winter, or an outbreak of disease can result in heavy losses of deer. When this happens, deer will remain scarce until range conditions improve.

Recurring periods of deer scarcity bring relief to the range. The surviving plants gradually recover their vigor, put on top growth, and accumulate food reserves. Perhaps for the first time in a number of seasons, they scatter seed crops. Seedlings become established. The older plants push out branches above the reach of deer or develop sucker and sprout growth, dense clumps of which provide some protection from browsing. Forage production goes into an upswing.

The length of the period of deer scarcity will vary with the nature of the range. On transitory forest range, for instance, the trees may grow out of reach of the deer and shade out the ground forage during the period of low numbers. The carrying capacity thus may remain low until logging, windthrow, or fire opens the forest canopy.

On stable range, where the predominant cover consists of shrubs, the period of deer scarcity may be shorter. Here, the deer may increase with improved forage production until they reach a level at which their feeding again depletes the food supply. Then the deer population again declines. Thus, the cycle of scarcity is repeated again and again.

CHAPTER 6

Food Preferences

ALL VEGETATION THAT GROWS ON DEER RANGE IS NOT DEER FOOD. TOO many people are unaware that many species of plants are worthless to deer. Some are fair foods, other good; few are excellent. A balanced diet for people must contain a variety of palatable foods. It is the same for deer. Few if any plants offer a complete diet in themselves. Ordinarily, deer thrive where they may choose freely among a variety of the plant species they like to eat.

Wild deer feed more heavily on some species of plants than on others, even where the latter are much more abundant. Game managers rate deer foods in accordance with the preferences the animals exhibit when presented a free choice of many plants. The ratings are based on the assumption that deer seek forages that are best for them (57).

There is some evidence, however, that deer do not always base their selection of food entirely on nutritional needs any more than humans do. In a Wisconsin test, for instance, wild-trapped deer were penned and fed different forages. Those on a diet of seven second-choice species actually lost less weight than those fed six species of preferred foods. While deer on third-choice and low-palatability diets lost more

Not all vegetation that grows on deer range is deer food.—*Photo courtesy Maine Department of Inland Fisheries and Game*

weight than those on second-choice or preferred foods, the study indicated that any of the diets could sustain deer over short yarding periods if available in unlimited amounts.

The highly preferred northern white cedar, however, when fed alone, did sustain deer for sixty days, while the low-preference balsam proved to be a starvation food, as did mixtures of jack pine and red oak. The Wisconsin investigators concluded that the species of plants that deer prefer are not necessarily the most nutritious and that a considerable variety of both coniferous and hardwood species is necessary for a complete diet (28).

The food-value findings in this study may well be true, although the principal point may be that deer, to maintain peak physical condition, must be free to eat when and what they want in any amount they need. One possible weakness in the study stems from the fact that wild deer appear able to choose more nutritious forage than that selected for their use by investigators (10). Also, browse that has been cut and sometimes stored for several days may possibly lose some of its nutritive value. This will be discussed later.

Livestock food studies have shown that cattle with access to stacks of hay grown on various sites feed first on those from the most fertile soils (13). Deer probably show the same selectivity. Workers in New York State found that deer browsed over 80 percent of the flowering dogwood plants in an oak woodland heavily fertilized with nitrogen; they took only 4 percent of the dogwood browse on an adjoining unfertilized area (128).

Conversely, deer appear able to detect vegetation of a harmful nature. In an Arizona feeding study, deer were offered poisonous plants along with other forages. Although the poisonous plants were species with which the deer were unfamiliar, they left them uneaten after a brief sampling (133).

A study of white-tailed deer in the South revealed a sharp decline in fawn production after the preferred browse species showed heavy use. In the longleaf-pine belt, adult deer were able to maintain themselves surprisingly well on second- and low-choice forages. But fawn production suffered from the very onset of heavy browsing and considerably before there was a significant use of the low-choice foods. The researchers concluded that whenever a highly palatable plant species that makes up more than 3 percent of the available vegetation is more than moderately browsed, the optimum carrying capacity of the range has been reached (70).

FOOD HABIT STUDIES

One way to learn feeding preferences is to examine contents of the rumens, the first stomachs, of dead deer. The amount and frequency of each kind of food present may be analyzed in the laboratory, tabulated, and compared with the kinds and quantity of the forage available on the range.

Another method is close examination of deer ranges. The makeup of the vegetation, the form classes (degree of hedging) of shrubs and trees, and the amount of current browsing on various plant species provide clues for preference ratings.

Mention has been made of studies with penned deer. In these projects, individual animals or groups of animals are confined for comparison under fully controlled conditions. Food and water intake, the amount that animals eat of various foods offered, body weight gain or loss under various diets, and similar information can be measured with considerable accuracy.

Still another method is direct observation of wild deer. The observer keeps a record of the time deer spend feeding on each kind of forage.

Table 2 shows a comparison of information obtained from rumen analysis. Here the average volume of sagebrush (30 percent) in the rumen samples exceeds that of bitterbrush (20 percent). Both items occurred in most of the stomachs collected—bitterbrush in 87 and sagebrush in 92 out of 100. But sagebrush is four times more abundant than bitterbrush on the range from which the deer were taken. It makes up 20 percent of the total vegetation compared to 5 percent for bitterbrush. Therefore, indications are that deer prefer bitterbrush over sagebrush. Although the latter is fourfold more abundant than bitterbrush, its average volume consumed by deer is not 400 percent greater, but only 50 percent greater than that of bitterbrush.

TABLE 2

COMPARISON OF DEER DIET DATA WITH VEGETATION COVER

Species	Volume in Stomach Samples	Frequency in Stomach Samples	Cover Composition
Bitterbrush	20%	87%	5%
Sagebrush	30%	92%	20%

Table 3 shows how analysis of food preferences can be made from range study alone. In this simplified example, sagebrush is four times as abundant as bitterbrush. But the browsing of bitterbrush is eight times heavier than that of sagebrush, indicating a clear preference of deer for the former.

TABLE 3

COMPARISON OF DEER BROWSING DATA WITH VEGETATION COVER

Species	Utilization	Shrubs Heavily Browsed	Composition on Range
Bitterbrush	48%	42%	5%
Sagebrush	6%	7%	20%

We should remember, however, that heavy use of a plant species on any one range does not necessarily mean that it is a first-class food.

It may simply be the best that is available on that particular range. It may be a food of necessity rather than of preference. But when the same plant species is used heavily on many deer ranges of different cover combinations, we are justified in accepting this as evidence of high preference.

As a deer herd increases beyond the optimum carrying capacity, demand for quality foods begins to exceed supply. Overbrowsing of preferred foods will cause a decline in forage production and so force the deer to feed on the less palatable forage species. Freedom of choice declines as the deer numbers rise, and the animals must subsist increasingly on low-value foods.

PALATABILITY

Sometimes, deer preference for a particular kind of plant appears to vary with its growing site. The palatability of plants of the same species can change in response to different soils and the degree of shading, burning, and other influences (18). At times, too, the presence or absence of other kinds of vegetation affects the acceptance of some species of plants by deer. Deer will feed sparingly on a diet of sagebrush alone. But they will eat large amounts of sagebrush if able to combine it with other forage species in their diets (8, 48, 160).

Colorado mule deer seek out rabbitbrush for food in one area; in another, only 100 miles distant, they ignore it (18). Wax myrtle is avidly eaten by white-tailed deer in North Carolina; those in Louisiana and Texas use it only lightly (92).

The amount of aromatic compounds known to chemists as "essential oils" in the foliage of a plant can influence its palatability (159). Mule deer in Utah browse heavily on junipers with low percentages of essential oils and neglect most of those with higher percentages (Table 4).

TABLE 4
AMOUNT OF ESSENTIAL OILS IN PREFERRED AND NONPREFERRED JUNIPER FOLIAGE

	Percentage of Essential Oils Present	
Species	In Trees Browsed by Deer	In Trees Not Browsed by Deer
Red juniper	1.8	2.3
Utah juniper	2.1	2.6

Several investigators suspect the high essential oil content of sagebrush as the principal inhibitor of its nutritional value to deer (8, 48,

Preferred browse species are easily recognized in northern deer yards by the priority and extent of deer use.—*Photo by Bill Cross, Maine Fish and Game Department*

160). Although it rates high in digestible protein and total digestible nutrients, deer do not seem able to maintain themselves on a straight sagebrush diet and often show signs of dietary upset (8).

Deer in Arizona seem to use conifers as a conditioning food or condiment rather than as a regular food. In one feeding experiment penned animals were offered fir, spruce, and pine. Often the animals would eat their fill of these forages, ignore them for ten days or so, and then make another full meal of one or more of them (133).

But in some regions conifers appear to be the regular preferred foods. Douglas fir is considered the most important single food of black-tailed deer in British Columbia (23). In the Northwest, generally, it is regarded as a starvation food in winter, but it is highly palatable and heavily used in spring and early summer. In Washington State it ranked seventh in a food perference study, below western hemlock and above western red cedar (14). White-tailed deer prefer yellow pine over Douglas fir in western Montana (1), and yellow pine is used heavily by deer on some ranges in South Dakota (82) and Wyoming (72).

Northern white cedar is one of the outstanding winter deer foods in the northeastern states, being both nutritious and highly palatable (4). Yew and hemlock, although inferior to white cedar, also appear to be preferred by northern whitetails. Pasture juniper is an important deer food in New England, and eastern red cedar is used by deer in New Hampshire, Massachusetts, and New York. Conversely, balsam, jack pine, and spruce fall into the starvation diet category (92).

As one moves from the northern forests into the central hardwood area and on into the southern states, the use of conifers by deer drops off sharply. Here the broad-leaved trees and shrubs take top billing. In some states—Missouri and Alabama, for example—we find deer again feeding on various species of pine and on eastern red cedar (92). In the longleaf pine belt of the South, loblolly and shortleaf pine are used by deer only on overbrowsed ranges (70). White-tailed deer in the Missouri Ozarks resort to the use of pine and cedar only during years of acorn shortage (39).

DEER DIETS

Deer eat many kinds of plants, but the bulk of their diet in any one area usually is made up of a relatively few favorite foods (Table 5). In the Great Basin, for instance, bitterbrush, curl-leaf mahogany, sagebrush, and juniper, along with herbaceous plants, make up 80 to 95 percent of the winter deer diet (100).

TABLE 5
PROMINENT DEER FORAGES IN VARIOUS REGIONS

Northern (28)	Central (92)	Southern (70, 52)
Apple	Pussytoe	Black titi
Black cherry	Blueberry	Flowering dogwood
Alternate-leaf dogwood	Greenbrier	Greenbrier
White cedar	Hazel	Red maple
Hemlock	Maple	Sumac
Red maple	Mountain laurel	Yellow poplar
Mountain ash	Sassafras	Tupelo gum
Sumac	Sumac	Sweetleaf
Yellow birch	Tulip poplar	White titi
Yew	Wild grape	Sassafras

TABLE 5—Continued

Texas (92)	Rocky Mountain	Great Basin (Summer) (162)
Acacia	Bearberry	Aspen
Black haw	Snowberry	Chokecherry
Greenbrier	Buckbrush	Clover
Forestiera	Chokecherry	Elderberry
Hackberry	Red osier	Gambel oak
Live oak	Oregon grape	Lupine
Persimmon	Sumac	Painted cup
Plum	Aspen	Penstemon
Sassafras	Tobacco brush	Snowberry
Sumac		
White ash		
Yellow jessamine		

Great Basin (Winter)	California Chaparral (169)
Bitterbrush	California bay
Curl-leaf mahogany	Chamise
Chokecherry	Chaparral pea
Gambel oak	Ceanothus
Sagebrush	Poison oak
Serviceberry	Scrub oak
Squaw carpet	Silk tassel
Tobacco brush	Wild grape

Rocky Mountain mule deer in Colorado feed primarily on ten species in summer; but 86 percent of their diet consists of serviceberry, chokeberry, and scrub oak (18). Deer on the Fish Lake range in Utah feed on 125 species of plants, but the bulk of their diet consists of no more than eight species each season (162). The minor items in the diet, of course, may provide some nutritional elements essential for a complete ration.

The important thing to remember about deer preference ratings is their variability. Even in one locality they may vary with the season of the year, the growth stages of the plants, and the changing composition of the plant cover. A plant species that is heavily used in one place may be ignored in another place or at another time. While preference ratings provide valuable information, they often must be modified for specific range situations.

CHAPTER 7

Nutritional Requirements of Deer

IF DEER ARE TO MAINTAIN THEMSELVES IN PEAK PHYSICAL CONDITION, their diets, like those of livestock or of people, must contain quality proteins, carbohydrates, sugars, fats, minerals, and vitamins.

Low energy intake as a result of insufficient food can slow down or even halt growth (including skeletal development) of an animal. It can also cause weight loss, reproductive failure, and a reduced resistance to diseases and parasites. Symptoms of low energy intake, however, often are confused by the simultaneous effect of insufficient proteins and other nutrients (76).

All animals need a certain minimum quantity of food to maintain themselves. Until they have this amount of food, they have no energy for growth or reproduction (126).

The effect of trying to increase animal numbers without increasing the food supply was demonstrated in a study conducted by the New Mexico Experiment Station. When the livestock were fed an adequate diet, cows averaged about 1000 pounds in weight and 90 percent produced calves. The calves weighed 400 pounds when weaned. But when the number of cattle was increased by 30 percent with the same

Big bucks like this Maine whitetail are a product of adequate nutrition from a balanced deer range.—*Photo courtesy Maine Fish and Game Department*

amount of food, the weight of the cows dropped to an average 700 pounds. Only about 40 percent of the cows produced calves, and most of the calves weighed 300 pounds or less at weaning. In the first case, 30 percent of the food went for calf production and 70 percent for body maintenance. In the second, 90 percent was required for body maintenance, and only 10 percent was recovered in calf production (76).

During the early 1940s the Nazi regime in Germany planned to use this food-energy principle to decimate the "non-Nordic" people in Europe. The plan was to feed these captive people just enough food to permit them to work, but not enough to encourage sexual activity. Such a program of slow starvation, the Nazis felt, would eliminate the undesired people within a relatively short time.

Adequate diet enables animals to ward off diseases. Studies in California show that sheep maintained on a plane of nutrition that results in the continuous growth of lambs resist ordinary stomach worms and intestinal parasites (83). Livestock growers know that a host of diseases can be prevented by adequate feeding. Bacteria that are ordinarily harmless to healthy animals often cause weakness and death in animals in poor condition (84).

That similar relationships occur in deer has been established by many studies throughout North America. In New York State investigators found dramatic differences in survival and reproductive success of white-tailed deer directly related to their food supplies. In the southern counties, with good range and adequate food, most of the deer survived the winter. This was in contrast to the situation on the northern ranges, where the number of deer exceeded the optimum capacity; their winter losses were heavy and frequent. The results of the study were similar to those found in the cow-feeding experiment in New Mexico. In his book, *Our Wildlife Legacy,* Durward Allen reported that 92 percent of the does became pregnant on the good range, compared to 78 percent on the poor range. In addition, 33 percent of the fawns were bred on the southern ranges, while only 4 percent became pregnant in the north (20).

Similar findings were made in Vermont, until recently a traditional "buck law" state. There the southern counties are overstocked with deer while those in the north have deer herds more in balance with their food supplies. A comparison was made between deer in northern and southern Vermont and those in Massachusetts, which until recently has provided no special protection for does. The results were revealing. Pregnancy rates of yearling does were 78 percent in northern Vermont, 61 percent in southern Vermont, and 92 percent in Massachusetts. The rates for mature does were 100 percent in northern Vermont, 88 percent in southern Vermont, and 99 percent in Massachusetts. Even more indicative of the effect of nutrition were the pregnancy rates in fawns. In Massachusetts 59 percent of the fawns were found to have bred; in Vermont the rate was practically nil—1 percent in the south and none at all in the north.

As if this were not enough, the number of embryos carried per 100 pregnant does in each region widened the disparity, particularly in the yearling class. There were 143 fetuses per 100 does in northern Vermont, 119 fetuses per 100 does in the south, and 180 in Massachusetts (46).

These figures show clearly the advantages of maintaining deer numbers at the optimum level in balance with their food supply. When they are analyzed they show that a hypothetical herd of does made up of 30 fawns, 20 yearlings, and 50 adults would, in one breeding season, produce 82 fawns in southern Vermont and 152 in Massachusetts. To put it another way, a herd of 55 does on good range will produce as many fawns as 100 on poor food.

EFFECTS OF DIET ON WEIGHT AND DEVELOPMENT

The effects of food supplies on the size and weight of deer also were demonstrated in Massachusetts. Undernourished animals on an over-populated and heavily browsed range averaged 32 pounds lighter in weight and 14 percent smaller in skeletal size than deer from range with adequate food (155).

Penned yearling whitetails fed a low-energy diet deficient in calcium, phosphorus, and protein in a Pennsylvania experiment were stunted in size and weight. They averaged 97 pounds at 15-16 months of age; those maintained on a full ration at the same time attained an average weight of 155 pounds at the same age. Moreover, the yearling bucks on the low-energy diet developed thin spike antlers five inches or less in length, while those on the full ration had antlers 12-15 inches long with three or four points (eastern count) (64).

In this experiment, deer placed on a restricted diet and shifted later to a complete ration made good recoveries in weight and antler growth, but none approached in condition those animals raised on a full diet. The daily food requirements of young deer of various sizes are shown in Table 6 (64). It will be seen that the need ranges from 3600 calories for a 50-pound fawn to 9900 calories for a 150-pound yearling (64).

TABLE 6

DAILY REQUIREMENTS OF QUALITY FOODS NEEDED BY DEER FOR OPTIMUM GROWTH (64)

Weight of Deer	Ration Needed in Pounds		
(in pounds)	Air-Dry	Green	Calories Required
50-60	2	4	3600
100	3-4	6-8	6300
150	5-6	10-12	9900

Many people believe that small deer are a product of inbreeding and that the introduction of new blood into a herd will remedy matters. But bucks taken as fawns from a poor range in Pennsylvania and raised to maturity on good food reached average weights nearly twice those of the wild bucks of the same stock on their home range (110).

Studies reported from Virginia show that antler size is governed largely by the quality of the food eaten by the buck while his antlers are developing. Antlers develop normally during spring and summer so long as forage is plentiful, even though that of the previous winter may have been inadequate. Antler development in yearling deer is a good indicator of the adequacy of the food supply, since antlers must be grown with whatever resources are available after basic body needs are met (27).

If the food supply is plentiful, most yearling white-tailed bucks should develop forked antlers during their second years. On the best ranges, spike yearlings average only about 5 percent of the herd; on

Antler development is governed by the quality of food while antlers are growing.—*Photo by Bill Cross, Maine Fish and Game Department*

average range, the percentage of spikes is around 30 percent. If spike yearlings make up more than 30 percent of the buck population, it indicates that there is an imbalance between the deer numbers and the food supply (77).

Winter is the critical period for fawn production even though, in most regions, the fawns are not dropped until late spring. As the fetus develops after the fall breeding season, does forced to winter on inadequate rations may lose about 30 percent of their young even in places where spring foods are plentiful. But if the spring forage also is inadequate, losses of young may run from 50 to as high as 90 percent (177).

Much the same information applies to the western deer. British

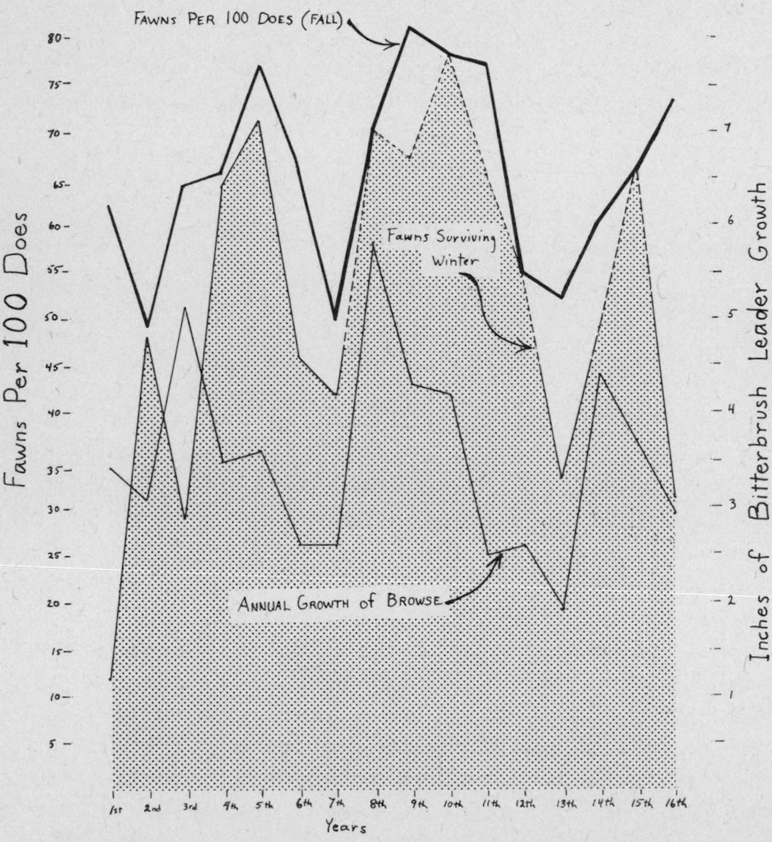

Relation of Annual Forage Supply to Fawn Production and Winter Fawn Survival on Doyle Deer Herd Unit, California, 1949-1965

Columbia blacktails raised in captivity on high-quality foods attained weights of over 200 pounds at two years of age; wild deer in that area commonly weigh around 100 pounds (25).

Mature black-tailed bucks taken on the Tillamook Burn in Oregon, during a period when forage plants were abundant and varied, dressed out at 210 pounds or more. On other nearby ranges, where food was less adequate, mature bucks of the same race averaged about 150 pounds (55).

Effects of food supplies on winter survival of mule deer were demonstrated dramatically in Utah in the bitter winter of 1948-49. Some deer herds lost 50 percent of their numbers, and fawn losses ran as high as 90 percent (104). Research workers at that time had three winter deer ranges under study. The general relationship between the amount of browse available and the winter losses in these three areas is shown in Table 7.

TABLE 7

DEER MORTALITY COMPARED WITH THE AMOUNT OF FOOD ON UTAH RANGE

Range	Amount of Browse Per Deer Day (in pounds)	Winter Mortality Percentage
South Oak Creek	57.8	9.5
Meadow Creek	12.5	26.0
Heaston	9.4	42.0

Normal mortality on the South Oak Creek range during the more usual winter in 1947-48 was 7 percent. The severe winter increased the rate of loss only 2.5 percent. But on the Heaston winter range, where browse was in short supply, 42 percent of the deer died (104).

Winter stress has more than an immediate effect on female deer. In British Columbia, even though the year was mild and favorable, each 100 does produced only 15 fawns after one severe winter (24). Much the same effect was reported in California. Fawn production was much reduced on six out of seven ranges under study after a severe winter (43).

Heavy parasite infestations and malnutrition go together; parasites are always present, awaiting only weakness in their animal hosts to reach serious numbers (99). There is a direct relationship between poor range conditions and losses of deer to parasites and diseases (89, 149). Parasitism tends to be greater in deer on heavily stocked ranges where the deer are forced to feed largely on grasses and consequently pick up immature parasites deposited on the ground in feces. Where deer are at lower densities or have access to a variety of browse species, they are far less subject to parasitism (176).

PROTEINS

Proteins are the building blocks of muscle, vital organs, hide, hair, and antlers. Protein deficiency can cause poor growth, loss of appetite, and failure in milk secretion and breeding periods in does. It also affects sexual potency through its effect on the pituitary gland, according to University of California workers. Menstrual periods become irregular or cease entirely in the female. In the male, lack of protein reduces sexual desire (76).

Complications in pregnancy, such as miscarriage, stillbirth, and premature birth, are more frequent where animals suffer from lack of sufficient protein. Mild to moderate protein deficiency renders young animals more susceptible to losses resulting from respiratory and gastrointestinal infections. Because of growth requirements, the need of young animals for protein is higher than that of adults; insufficient protein intake during the early growing period can result in reduced adult stature (102a).

The protein needs of animals are made up of two kinds: (1) a basal amount below which health and growth are impaired and (2) an additional amount to provide for stress, such as minor disease, pain, and anxiety. Overpopulation of animals results in competition and conflict and this increases day-to-day stresses. A diet adequate in protein for an optimum population may become deficient when the number of animals on a unit reaches the population ceiling. There is evidence also that the stress of extreme cold leads to increased protein deficiency, because the muscle tissues are sapped to provide the needs of vital organs. The result is emaciation and weakness. A lack of sufficient total food, as well as of necessary vitamins and minerals, will result in a lower utilization of dietary protein and thus compound the problem (102a).

Crude protein content is a good index of the food value of a plant. A crude protein level of 7 percent is required to maintain western deer in most situations where an adequate supply of palatable browse is available (9). Along the Oregon coast, losses of deer occur whenever the crude protein content drops much below 6 percent (55).

In Pennsylvania, however, feeding trials showed that a crude protein level of from 13 to 16 percent was needed for the optimum growth of young white-tailed deer (64). And in Michigan, studies indicated that even 16 percent is insufficient to support maximum weight gains in buck whitetail fawns; 20 percent was required, even though 12.7 percent seemed adequate for young does (184).

California researchers determined the chemical composition of eight browse species; those most preferred by deer showed a higher crude protein content than did the less preferred species (78).

Factors other than protein content, of course, affect the adequacy of foods for deer. White cedar, one of the best northern browses, contains less crude protein than several other kinds of browse, such as balsam, which ranks as a starvation food (4). Deer in California do better on a straight winter diet of bitterbrush than they do on a sagebrush diet, even though the latter contains considerably more protein (8).

The amount of crude protein in plants reaches a high during the spring growing season and falls off to a low during dormancy—in some species much lower than in others. At times fluctuations in the protein content of various kinds of plants cause changes in the diets of deer. Preferred forage plants that maintain high crude protein levels during their dormancy periods usually, but not always, are the most important on a deer range.

Deer have the ability to step up the protein content in their diets by selecting the most nutritious parts of the available plants. Of course, this is possible only where there is enough preferred forage to permit choice. Stomach samples taken from black-tailed deer on chaparral brush range in California averaged 17.6 percent crude protein. When investigators carefully selected twig ends of browse species in portions similar to those in the rumen samples, the mixture averaged only 6.9 percent crude protein. These findings were repeated in studies of Rocky Mountain mule deer taken from Great Basin range cover types. The values averaged 17.2 percent crude protein in browse eaten by deer and 7.1 percent in that collected by the researchers (10).

When it is remembered that a full protein diet enables a ruminant to use roughage foods efficiently, the effect of imbalance between deer numbers and food supply becomes apparent. The competition among deer, the pressure of high demand on a limited food supply, and the need of deer to use coarser and less desirable foods to fill their bellies, all lessen the opportunity for an animal to select high-protein forage. And once an animal is denied adequate protein, it becomes increasingly less able to digest low-quality forage. Thus the animal on overpopulated range is caught in a vicious circle of browse depletion and malnutrition often ending in premature death.

SALT

Opinions differ on the need for salt by wild deer. Big game animals got along well with only natural sources of salt in primitive times. And no clear-cut case for the need of a salt supplement can be made today (131).

There is considerable evidence that the taste for free salt is acquired, both by humans and by animals. It may be a condiment—a flavoring or relish—rather than an essential element of diet. Those holding this view say that only small quantities of sodium chloride are required to maintain health, and these are present in many natural foods (76).

On the other hand, early investigators pointed out that the need for free salt can vary with the chemical contents of the local food and water supply and with physiological differences between individual animals (19).

Research workers at the Wisconsin Agricultural Research Experiment Station deprived confined dairy cows of free salt. Although the general health of the cows remained sound from less than a month to more than a year, all eventually suffered breakdown, usually at calving or soon thereafter. The animals lost appetite and weight, declined in milk production, and developed a haggard appearance with lackluster eyes and rough coats. When salt was provided, they recovered rapidly. A steer or dry cow probably would not have suffered on the ration provided in this test, which was calculated to provide ¾ ounce of sodium chloride daily (19).

The need of beef cattle for salt appears to be low. California investigators who studied this, however, recommended that free salt be provided to cattle because of its value as a condiment (76). Livestock use more salt while on green than on dry feed. Prolonged rain, however, can leach nearly all common salt out of dry vegetation.

Salt consumption by deer is affected by the nature of the forage, air temperature, and exercise. In Arizona, penned deer were found to eat 1/10 pound per month in summer and 1/20 pound in winter (133).

If deer do require salt, a deficiency of the mineral is most apt to occur on most ranges in spring, when the animals turn to fresh green herbaceous foods, and for five or six weeks after fawning.

Heavy eating of free salt by semistarved deer on low protein diets can be harmful and aggravate their edematous condition. In extreme cases, it may hasten death (127).

There is a popular belief that adding sulphur to salt will help keep animals that eat it free of parasites, such as ticks and fleas. This has never been demonstrated; any animal that ate enough sulphur to repel external parasites probably would die of sulphur poisoning.

MINERALS AND TRACE ELEMENTS

During the 1950s red deer in Austria began to cause serious damage to forests by heavy browsing and by peeling bark from tree trunks. Forest managers tried reducing the animals, improving natural feeding areas, and providing winter food supplements. These measures helped reduce the damage, but not below a tolerable level. But when supplementary foods containing minerals and trace elements were made available, the bark peeling dropped to acceptable levels. Moreover, fawn productivity increased by at least 20 percent and antler development improved (119).

Evidence from New Hampshire indicates that deer may use "licks" not so much because of a craving for salt as for other essential elements in the soil. This was verified by the death of fawns denied access to soil. On some ranges it is not uncommon to find droppings composed entirely of soil particles (86a).

The effect of nutritional deficiencies on health, size, and productivity of deer points out the vital importance of a complete diet. The natural checks that reduce the productivity of deer when the animals increase above the optimum carrying capacity of their range tend to protect forage plants from decimation. But from the human standpoint, this natural culling is far from ideal because it is wasteful. As plants lose their vigor and start to decline, the productivity of the range falls off. When the food supply becomes inadequate, fawn production drops below potential, fawn survival declines, adult mortality increases, and heavy losses of deer occur periodically. Waste of this kind is difficult to justify in the face of high demand for products of the land—including hunting experiences. Since it is not feasible to maintain surplus deer by artificial feeding, the only alternative is to keep the deer population in balance with its natural food supply through the removal of surplus animals.

CHAPTER 8

Characteristics of Deer Forage

WE HAVE ALREADY STRESSED SEVERAL FACTS ABOUT DEER FORAGE. Different kinds of plants change in food value month by month throughout the year. The species of browse plants or herbs that are important deer forage in one season may be next to worthless in another. Foods that rate high in chemical analysis actually may be of poor quality either because of the presence of essential oils or because of other factors that affect their palatability or inhibit their usefulness.

University of California investigators report that the "value of individuals foods depends not only on the amount of digestible nutrients they contain, but also on their palatability, their physical effect, and their use with other foods to furnish the quantity and quality of protein, essential minerals and vitamins necessary to form a complete ration" (76).

There are a few forage species that can serve as single-item diets and sustain deer for at least several weeks as, for instance, bitterbrush (8) or northern white cedar (92). But investigators are unanimous that deer need mixtures of several forages to maintain good condition and maximum survival.

Studies of the response of sheep to native foods in Utah indicate that forage species in mixed diets were digested more efficiently than when eaten as single-item diets (21). This is especially important to remember when range vegetation is being modified for livestock or other purposes. On deer winter ranges, treatments that result in destruction of browse mixture and substitution of single-species stands of grass over extensive areas are not in the best interest of deer.

Deer need a variety of food plants to maintain their health and vigor. It follows logically that the best deer ranges usually contain mixtures of rather diverse plant communities, from grasses and sedges to mast-producing trees.

HERBACEOUS PLANTS

Herbaceous vegetation includes the grasses and grasslike sedges and rushes and broad-leaved herbs, such as clovers and dandelions. The latter are commonly called *forbs* by ecologists. All three classes of herbs are important in the diet of deer.

Some reports from the northeastern states indicate that deer feed heavily on grasses only in areas where overpopulations occur (92). It

Acorns, produced by oaks of many species over a broad range, are valuable deer foods, wherever they are available.—*Photo by W. G. Macgregor, California Department of Fish and Game*

is natural, of course, for deer to eat available grasses when and where other more preferred forage is scarce or absent. But, in many areas, deer feed on grasses by choice during certain times of the year, even where other foods are abundantly available.

Trippensee, in his book *Wildlife Management,* points out that white-tailed deer begin to graze with the first appearance of lush new grasses and herbs in early spring and continue to use these plants, along with browse, as long as they retain their palatability (175). In the Missouri Ozarks, grasses and grasslike plants form a major part of the spring diet of whitetails, along with flower buds, catkins, and twig tips as these break winter dormancy (39). On Utah's Fish Lake range, bluegrass represents 84 percent of the spring food of mule deer, even though it makes up less than 7 percent of the available forage (162).

Grasses, either green or dry, are acceptable to Arizona deer at all seasons, and forbs also are an important part of their diet (133). Black-tailed deer in British Columbia feed throughout the summer on a mixture of grasses, forbs, and browse (147). Joseph Dixon, former biologist of the National Park Service, concluded after years of observation that "some grass is eaten whenever it is available . . . at certain seasons, fresh, green grass forms as high as 90 percent of the food eaten by mule deer" (50).

A study of the Doyle mule deer herd in Nevada and California indicated that grasses may have accounted for the difference between good and poor deer winter survival. A principal difference between kinds of food taken in mild as compared to severe winters was the higher volume of grasses consumed, from January through March (109). South Dakota whitetails follow this same pattern of winter use of grass.

Grasses are used more heavily by deer than most early research workers realized.—*Photo by W. G. Macgregor, California Department of Fish and Game*

During open winters, grasses make up 13 percent of their diet but only 5 percent in winters with deeper snows (82).

Both annual and perennial grasses, when green, are high in water, protein, and mineral content, and low in crude fiber. During active growth, grasses have the characteristics of a concentrated food rich in protein (76). After a winter spent on low-quality foods, deer turn eagerly to new grass. But in its early growth stage, grass has a high moisture content that makes it difficult for the animals to derive a full diet from it. Deer in poor condition sometimes die after a change from browse to grass.

Protein content declines rapidly in grasses as they approach maturity. In addition, they lose much of their energy value and mineral content as they cure after setting seed. Dry grass, because of high fiber content and low digestibility, furnishes little more than maintenance requirements for cattle, and presumably for deer, even when supplemented with protein and minerals (76). Those grasses that retain their seed at maturity, such as soft chess and Indian ricegrass, maintain higher food values than those that do not.

Perennial grasses, generally, are superior to annuals. They start growing earlier, stay green longer, and withstand drought better.

Deer prefer fresh, green grass that is free of stubble. They will often move out of preserves into adjacent livestock pastures where the cattle have cropped back the summer growth. They use such grasslands more heavily than those in which stubble from the previous year is mixed with the new green grass (120). This may help to explain the lower preference by deer for grasses in some regions.

The use of grasses by deer peaks shortly after the onset of active spring growth and falls off rapidly after the broad-leaved herbs appear. The forbs, in turn, lose importance with the development of new succulent browse, although they remain prominent in the deer diet throughout summer. Their use is heaviest when late-growing herbs are available in the succulent growth stage (112).

Legumes are important summer foods. A study in Utah showed that clovers made up 40 percent of the food eaten by mule deer during July, although they represent only 7 percent of the available forage. Lupine made up 57 percent of the food eaten in browse cover type and 27 percent of that eaten in aspen cover, although it constituted no more than 6 percent of the available food in both types (162).

One of the important factors in higher fawn production by black-tailed deer on managed chaparral brush range in California appears to be the availability of herbaceous forage. In undisturbed chapparral, herbs made up about 5 percent of the year-long diet. After manage-

Legumes are important summer deer foods. This stand of clover in Maine was established by seeding a logging road.—*Photo courtesy Maine Fish and Game Department*

ment converted the dense brush to a mixture of grasses, forbs, and shrubs, use of herbaceous foods jumped to 35 percent of the total diet. Significantly, production of fawns on this range rose from 71 per 100 adult does in undisturbed brush to 145 per 100 in the managed shrublands (169).

Rain leaches most of the water-soluble carbohydrates and minerals, including salt, from the dry herbs. Under such conditions the plants lose much of their food value. Extended wet weather may damage them further by encouraging the development of molds and other agents of decomposition (76).

Deer probably seldom deplete herbaceous cover except where it occurs in limited and scattered stands. The condition of grasslands and meadows in national parks and other places where livestock are excluded seems to bear this out. Excessive selection grazing by overpopulations of deer can reduce some of the most palatable species of plants; but even under such conditions, deer-feeding alone practically never denudes the soil. In fact, the overuse of browse plants by deer often encourages the development of grasses on areas where deer are the only grazers.

On a range in Utah, where deer were fed supplementary foods, overbrowsing caused hedging of the juniper, mahogany, bitterbrush, and staghorn sumac on areas adjacent to the feeding grounds; young plants were eaten to the ground. Even species with low preference rating, such as rabbitbrush and maple, were heavily browsed. And yet, the native grasses, principally bluegrass, increased on areas not grazed by livestock (51). On a second range in Utah used exclusively by deer, perennial grasses were more vigorous and abundant and forbs much more prominent than those on adjacent areas shared by livestock and deer (157).

In Rocky Mountain National Park, heavy browsing by deer killed much of the sagebrush and "high-lined" the ponderosa pine; but slender wheatgrass increased and replaced much of the depleted browse (141).

On the other hand, when deer use is superimposed by domestic livestock, it may well contribute to the depletion of herbaceous plants on the range.

BROWSE

Browse consists of shoots, twigs, leaves, needles, catkins, and flower buds produced by trees, shrubs, and woody vines. Fruits and nuts are called mast.

Deer browse more than they graze, except—on most ranges—during spring and early summer. They use the products of woody plants heavily in late summer and autumn; and in winter, when grass is scarse or unavailable, browse constitutes the bulk of their diet.

The food value of browse differs with the plant species. As with grasses, it is highest in protein, water, and mineral content and lowest in crude fiber during the active growing period. At maturity, its protein content usually is higher than that of mature grasses or forbs (76) and its crude fiber content markedly lower (71). The food value of many browse plants, however, is quite low during late fall and winter.

A critical period for deer in California's chapparral brush ranges occurs in late summer and early autumn, when the food value of a majority of the browse plants is low. Once the fall rains stimulate new growth of browse and herbaceous vegetation, the diet of the deer improves. Killing frosts, however, sometimes knock out this food supply during the winter.

The nutritive value of browse, like that of grass, may be very low during its initial succulent growth stage. Although chemical analyses usually show high percentages of crude protein and other nutrients during this period, the amount available to deer is masked. Chemical analysis is based on air-dry or oven-dry weights. But during the initial growing period, green weights are several times the dry weights for equal volume because of the high moisture content in the green browse. Thus, in early spring a deer paunchful of green browse has much less food value than chemical analysis of the forage would indicate (9).

Hundreds of important browse species occupy the ranges of the white-tailed and mule deer. We shall examine briefly only the relationships between deer and three major genera—sagebrush, bitterbrush, and the oaks.

Sagebrush occurs in many species throughout the West. Some are important supplementary deer foods; others are worthless to deer. Big sagebrush and black sagebrush are among the most abundant and are important foods on many winter mule deer ranges in the Great Basin. Bud sage is less common; but where it occurs, it is a valuable food, in spite of its thorny character. Silver sagebrush has little value as deer food.

Big sagebrush contains about half as much protein and twice as much fat and carbohydrate as green alfalfa (73, 160). In chemical composition, black sagebrush is similar to big sagebrush (21). The crude protein content of big sagebrush browse varies from 18 percent in April to 9 percent in March (9). But certain essential oils in the foliage of sagebrush seem to make it toxic to deer when they eat it in quantity.

Bitterbrush is one of the most important western deer foods (90). Browse from this species is used by deer during every month of the year, except possibly April or May on some ranges where grasses and forbs make up most of the spring diet. Bitterbrush is not outstandingly high in crude protein content, which ranges from 15 percent in May to 7 percent in March (9, 76).

In some areas, deer reportedly prefer sagebrush to bitterbrush in their midwinter diet (109, 112, 158). Whether this is a sign of preference or of necessity after the more nutritious parts of the bitterbrush have been eaten is not known (2). But it is true that the protein content of bitterbrush is lower than that of sagebrush during the period from January through March.

It may be significant that a study of California's Verdi winter range showed that deer in that area browsed on bitterbrush throughout the winter (59). Bitterbrush is more abundant there than sage, and the average cropping by deer during the study tended to be light. Table 8 compares the percentages of bitterbrush and sagebrush in stomach samples of deer from this range to those from the adjacent Doyle winter range, where bitterbrush is relatively less abundant but heavily browsed (112). The prominence of bitterbrush in the winter diet in the Verdi range contrasts sharply with its use on the Doyle range, where sagebrush overshadowed it from December through May.

California investigators found no change in the digestibility of sage brush and bitterbrush in samples collected throughout the winter. But they found extreme differences in the response of captive deer to these browse species when offered as single-species diets. The deer ate 2.2 pounds of air-dry bitterbrush per hundredweight but only 0.6

TABLE 8

VOLUME OF BITTERBRUSH AND SAGEBRUSH IN DEER DIET ON LIGHTLY STOCKED AS COMPARED TO HEAVILY STOCKED RANGE*

	Lightly Stocked (59)		Heavily Stocked (112)	
Month	Bitterbrush	Sagebrush	Bitterbrush	Sagebrush
September	34.8	Trace	60.2	—
November	40.6	9.8	51.6	11.8
December	15.0	1.0	20.5	26.9
January	23.4	16.8	10.0	64.9
February	25.8	35.2	9.9	53.4
April	3.2	18.6	4.8	34.4
May	60.6	21.6	14.7	44.4

pounds of sagebrush. Deer fed a straight diet of sagebrush with crude protein contents of from 11.2 to 13.8 percent lost more than a pound a day. But they maintained weight and appeared satisfied on diets of bitterbrush with crude protein contents of from 8.1 to 9.6 percent. The study showed that bitterbrush alone will support deer for several weeks during winter with only slight loss of weight (8).

Bitterbrush is a poor producer of forage on overbrowsed range, although individual plants can withstand considerable abuse. Under prolonged overbrowsing, the shrub loses vigor and produces sparse new growth and little viable seed (90). But its browsing tolerance is much greater than that of sagebrush. On study plots in Rocky Mountain National Park, 85 percent of the sagebrush but only 35 percent of the bitterbrush plants were killed by overbrowsing by deer and elk in a four-year period (141).

Bitterbrush requires more moisture than sagebrush, and, consequently, is much more susceptible to damage during long dry periods. Heavy browsing increases the moisture requirements of all shrubs. It can cause the loss of bitterbrush plants on overstocked deer ranges during dry years.

Bitterbrush will sprout after burning in some areas, particularly in the northern parts of its range; but this is not true everywhere. Within the Great Basin, a hot fire may eliminate bitterbrush from the burned area for a long time.

Oaks, which occur in many recognized species over a broad range, provide both mast and browse for white-tailed and mule deer. Acorns are especially valuable foods, and deer eat them in quantity whenever

*In percentage volume of stomach samples

they are available.

All acorns are low in protein and minerals but high in fats and starches (76). Dixon reported that California mule deer eat only the meat of acorns, carefully separating it from the hull before chewing it to a fine pulp (50). This is not always the case, however, since kernels and hulls are often found in rumen content analyses. Acorn kernels have much higher food value than hulls. Blue oak acorns, for example, average 5 percent protein, while the hulls average only 3 (71). This is some indication that hulls in the diet may actually depress the digestibility of proteins.[1] Food values of the kernels of five species of western oaks, determined by study at the University of California, are given in Table 9 (76).

TABLE 9
COMPARISON OF CHEMICAL VALUES OF DIFFERENT KINDS OF WESTERN ACORNS (76)

Species	Crude Protein (percent)	Fat (percent)	Tannin (percent)
Black oak	4.3	14.7	1.9
Scrub oak	2.6	4.3	4.1
Blue oak	3.5	5.8	2.6
Water oak	3.1	5.5	3.2
Interior live oak	3.5	17.8	5.0

In feeding tests, beef cattle lost weight on diets of acorns and dry range forage, a low-value food. The addition of a protein supplement checked this trend (76). Whether deer on diets of acorns react similarly when deprived of green browse is not known.

In the northern forests of the East, oaks generally are of minor importance in the diets of white-tailed deer, largely because of their scarcity. Deer browse on the available oaks and seek out their acorns in good mast years. But as soon as deep snow covers the ground, acorns disappear from their diet (92).

Farther south, in the central and southern regions, oak browse assumes medium importance and acorns prime importance as deer foods. In fact, during good mast years, acorns may make up 80 percent of the total food in fall and early winter (80, 92).

The great variety of oaks present in eastern hardwood forests makes complete acorn failures infrequent; usually one species or another will produce acorns in most years. A stand of 27 oaks per acre averaging 10 inches in trunk diameter will produce an average yield of nearly

[1]Bissell, Harold. 1969. Personal communication.

150 pounds of acorns. This can double or triple in good production years (53). In the central Appalachians, post-blackjack oak types produce an average of 90 pounds of deer browse per acre in the seedling stage and up to 190 pounds per acre at maturity (29).

White, water, willow, and laurel oaks are the most important producers of deer browse among the oaks in the South (80). Evergreen oaks, such as live and shin oak, are reported to supply the great bulk of deer forage in Texas (92).

Oaks also are important deer foods on many western ranges. The partially expanded new leaves of blue oak in spring average about 30 percent crude protein (151). In summer, deer feed on both sprouts and leaves. Even the cured leaves of California black oak are eaten by deer after the rains have softened them (50). Scrub oak is an important deer food throughout winter.

Leaves of the mountain white oak seem to have higher food value than those of other species present in California. Their crude protein content ranges from 19 percent in August to 14 percent in October (76). The value of blue oak leaves ranges from 14.5 percent in May to 10.5 percent in September (71).

Many of the western oaks rate high in palatability of their browse to deer. Black oak and scrub oak are excellent; canyon live oak, interior live loak, blue oak, and valley white oak all rate as good (50). Gambel oak is an especially important browse species in the Great Basin, and turbinella oak is browsed regularly by deer in the Southwest.

The month-by-month use of oak browse by black-tailed deer from October to May on one range in California is shown in Table 10.

TABLE 10

PLACE OF OAKS IN DEER WINTER DIET (113)

Species	O	N	D	J	F	M	A	M
Blue oak	15%	15%	11%	Trace	1%	Trace	—	Trace
Scrub oak	2%	—	2%	31%	9%	—	Trace	62%
Oregon oak	8%	—	—	—	—	—	—	—
Black oak	28%	—	—	—	—	—	6%	21%
Interior live oak	—	Trace	—	—	—	—	—	—
Other	Trace	—	—	Trace	20%	—	—	—
Total	53%	15%	13%	31%	30%	Trace	6%	83%

The amount taken ranges from a trace in March, when the animals begin turning heavily to green herbaceous forage, to 83 percent of their total food in May (113).

CHAPTER 9

Supplemental Feeding

WHENEVER AN OVERPOPULATION OF DEER OCCURS, SOMEONE ALWAYS asks, "Why not feed the deer?"

It is not for lack of adequate supplemental food that state game departments are reluctant to start feeding programs. Both mule and white-tailed deer in Arizona have been maintained in excellent physical condition on diets consisting of alfalfa leaves mixed in equal quantity with a combination of rolled barley, shelled corn, and whole oats (133). Young whitetails in New York State thrived on mixtures of alfalfa hay and cracked corn or whole corn, digesting them as easily as goats of the same age. In the same study, deer gained weight rapidly when fed a cake made up of 45 parts of molasses and 55 parts by weight of chopped soybeans. The investigators suggested that a cake of this kind could be used to supplement the diet of wild deer during emergencies. A 50-pound cake will feed eight deer for about 10 days (124).

In Wisconsin, research showed that good alfalfa hay in unlimited quantities would sustain deer through their average yarding period. A mixture of 60 percent balsam browse (a starvation food by itself) and 40 percent alfalfa hay gave satisfactory results; but deer fed unlimited quantities of alfalfa meal pellets lost less weight than when on any other diet tested. These pellets have the added advantages of being easy to handle, and they can be used with little waste (28).

Mule deer fed a 60:40 percent mixture of alfalfa hay and Purina pellets in Utah lost little weight over a 67-day period. Alfalfa hay was found to be an adequate emergency food, when the deer also have access to fair to good browse plants; deer eat such plants regardless of the availabliity of supplemental foods (51). A comparable study in Colorado determined that alfalfa pellets were highly nutritious and palatable to Rocky Mountain mule deer (48).

But although suitable supplemental foods are available, the strong case against supplemental feeding of wild deer rests on economics and practicality and on potential damage to the range.

When deer numbers grow out of balance with natural food supplies, losses to causes related to malnutrition place a rough ceiling on the population. This is nature's way of taking care of surplus deer and achieving a balance between the plants and the plant-eaters. From the human point of view, it is far from ideal, since it creates waste of animals. But it is preferable to the destruction by overbrowsing of the native deer-food plants.

Supplemental feeding removes this natural check. If it is successful, more deer are carried through the winter to exert further pressures on the native plants. Heavier supplemental rations then will be needed the next year to support the increased population, which will further damage the range foods. Eventually, when natural forage plants are destroyed, the deer will become entirely dependent on artificial foods. Before this point is reached, however, the cost of the feeding program usually will become exorbitant.

But even limited artificial feeding programs are not universally effective. Most state game departments that have tried have reported losses—sometimes heavy losses—in spite of using foods that provide an adequate diet to penned deer.

These deaths probably result from the inability of the animals to adjust to abrupt changes in diet. Livestock often suffer and sometimes die when shifted from dry to succulent foods or when changed rapidly from range forage to grain or concentrates. Sudden dietary changes are especially dangerous to starved animals. The losses seem to be related to an imbalance of the microorganisms (commensals) in the rumen, or first stomach, that are essential to digestion (83).

Commensals are benign, bacterialike organisms whose feeding activities in the rumen of deer and other ruminants help break down raw foods as the first step in digestion. Different foods are attacked by dif-

Winter feeding of deer, in the long run, usually aggravates rather than corrects situations of this kind. In the spring of 1964 State Game Commission biologists in Oregon counted more than 200 dead deer in the vicinity of feeding stations maintained by citizens in Baker County.—*Photo by Oregon Game Commission*

ferent species of commensals in number as needed to accommodate new foods. When changes in diet, as from low to high-protein forage, are sudden rather than gradual, the needed species of commensals may not be present in sufficient numbers. In their absence, toxic substances, such as ammonia, form in the rumen, causing extreme distress and sometimes death (68a).

Supplemental feeding usually is started only after deer begin to starve. Starved animals tend to gorge themselves when confronted suddenly with an abundance of acceptable food. Overeating leads to the formation of gas in the rumen and causes bloat. Informed livestock growers overcome this difficulty by accommodating their animals gradually to any new foods. Salt mixed with supplemental food also tends to limit the amount an animal can eat. But there are times when a high salt intake can be dangerous—when animals are on either a potassium-deficient or protein-deficient diet. Potassium deficiency rarely occurs on deer ranges, but protein deficiency is common on most overbrowsed winter ranges, where supplemental feeding is most likely to be tried. A diet heavy in salt under such conditions can aggravate the abnormal generation and accumulation of body fluids, known as edema, that often occurs in deer on protein-deficient diets (127).

Artificial or supplementary feeding of deer is used successfully and commonly in game preserves in Europe, where the herds are relatively localized and intensively managed, and where game populations are regulated closely. There, feeding is started early enough to permit the animals to accommodate to the supplementary diet long before they are subjected to servere winter stresses. But conditions in Europe are a far cry from those in North America, where the deer herds are scattered over thousands of square miles of winter range and subjected to a comparatively loose system of management.

Under North American conditions, even emergency feeding of a small proportion of the deer can be prohibitively costly. Locating the groups of deer that need feeding and transporting food to them, often over many miles of rough and snowy terrain, are difficult tasks even with the advent of the snowmobile and helicopter. In the winter of 1942, the Colorado Fish and Game Department spent $38,000 to feed the Gunnison mule deer herd. Yet, around 5000 of the deer died that winter, practically all with their stomachs full of alfalfa and food concentrates. In one canyon, research workers counted 253 carcasses on a 40-acre tract (99).

Under our present level of management, supplemental feeding is impractical. But it is entirely possible that changing concepts of wildlife values may alter this in the future, at least, on some deer ranges. When and if public demand, new and flexible laws, and increased funds and manpower make intensive deer management possible, regular feeding may become a standard management procedure. But, today, except for short-term emergencies on a few ranges, it is out of the question.

Meanwhile, many game departments have developed plans for feeding deer during true emergency situations. Most of these plans wisely provide for use of native browse, rather than artificial supplements, to feed the deer. Deer ranges contain an abundance of palatable shrubs and trees that have grown out of reach of the animals. The cutting of mature aspen, northern white cedar, and other valuable browse species growing near deer yards, during critical winter periods can bring deer through an emergency in the East. The Minnesota Plan for Emergency Winter Care of Deer calls for cutting of tall shrubs and the culling of hardwoods of low commercial value, as well as poor-quality cedar, around deer yards during periods of very heavy snowfall. Such woody plants as mountain maple, elderberry, dogwood, sumac, willow and the like are cut at snow line. Their tops provide emergency food immediately, and the stump sprouts develop to offer an enhanced deer food supply for the future (150a). Similar plans for emergency feeding of deer have been developed by other states.

CHAPTER 10

Herd Units and Seasonal Ranges

MANY STATES NOW MANAGE THEIR DEER ON THE BASIS OF UNITS. SOME emphasize the hunting unit, dividing the state into logical hunting areas with well-defined boundaries. Others emphasize the biological unit—the territory occupied by an individual deer herd.

The biological unit for migratory deer (such as the mule deer over much of its range) consists of a winter range or a group of related winter ranges or yards and their complementary spring, summer, and fall ranges where the majority of the animals that use the winter range spend the balance of the year (118). Some of the deer may roam widely, crossing one or more watersheds to summer outside the home unit, but most of the animals will summer within watersheds adjacent to the areas on which they winter (5, 51, 75).

Nonmigratory deer usually are managed on the basis of topographic or land-use units within which general range conditions and management problems are relatively uniform (118).

Where climate and food, water, and cover permit or topography dictates, deer may spend their entire lives on a limited territory. During the heat of the day in summer, nonmigratory deer will move to north

The summer and winter ranges of mule deer may be separated by as much as 100 miles.—*Photo courtesy U.S. Forest Service*

slopes where the cover is heavier, vegetation greener, and temperatures cooler. But they will feed during the evening, night, and early morning on areas where the choicest foods occur. Conversely, when winter comes, deer favor the south slopes during the daylight hours, where the rays of the sun are warmest and where the first plant growth of the year provides attractive food (169).

Migratory deer, on the other hand, follow the developing vegetation each spring from the low winter ranges to summer ranges on the highlands, sometimes for distances up to 100 miles (100). The reverse migration occurs in the fall as freezing weather, frosted forage, or snow make the higher slopes uninhabitable. In most situations the winter range occupies a much more limited area than the summer range. Animals that wander over several hundred thousand acres in the warmer months usually concentrate in a much smaller territory because of snow or other unfavorable conditions during the winter.

Evidence of deer overpopulation usually appears first on the winter ranges. Not only is the area smaller, but the green forage of spring and summer declines both in nutritive value and abundance as the plants cure or enter dormancy. The result is a deficiency both in quality and quantity of available foods. For this reason, the condition of the winter range usually is the key to the number of deer the biological unit can support.

No matter how abundant and lush the forage on the summer range may be, the number of migratory deer that can survive through winter is limited to that which the winter concentration areas, or yards, can sustain. For this reason, the winter range usually forms the basis for management. If the winter range can be maintained in good condition, the much larger summer range, unless subjected to damage from other causes, usually will care for itself.

Once game managers fully understood the importance of winter range, it was natural for them to focus their attention on such areas. More recently, the summer range has received detailed study. It has been found that summer range may be a limiting factor in some instances either because of natural deficiencies or because of use by livestock. Biologists in Utah and Idaho have concluded that good summer range is essential for maximum deer production. Yearling mule deer bucks on a severely depleted Utah summer range weighed 28 percent less and female fawns 35 percent less than those on good summer range in Idaho. One hundred does on the Utah range produced only 119 fetuses, while a comparable number in Idaho produced 185 (106).

A similar study in Colorado confirmed these findings. It determined that good summer range is important to the health and vigor of deer. An abundance of high-quality summer foods is needed by lactating does and enhances the survival of their fawns. In addition, it permits the animals to attain peak physical condition needed for optimum breeding and fetus development and to face the rigors of winter. The Colorado workers concluded that a decline in the quality and quantity of forage on the summer range will be followed almost inevitably by a decrease in deer numbers and a decline in the physical condition of the animals (48).

These and other studies (101, 106, 169) show that high fawn production and survival to early winter are good indicators of the adequacy of the summer range. If high conception rates are combined

The scarcity or abundance of forage in the wintering areas has an important bearing on the year-round health of the deer.—*Photo courtesy Maine Department of Inland Fisheries and Game*

with low summer fawn survival, a winter-spring food problem may be causing absorption of embryos, slinking of fetuses, or birth of weak, short-lived fawns. The condition of the winter range also should be suspect if a high summer fawn survival is followed by heavy winter losses.

CHAPTER 11

Predation and Competition

DEER EXIST ON EACH RANGE AS MEMBERS OF AN INTERRELATED AND interdependent community of plants and animals. The animals of any area are as much a part of the environment as are food, water, and vegetation. They usually are present in wide variety and in complex relationships. Individually, each species may be helpful, harmful, or of no known significance to deer. Of the multitude of vertebrate and invertebrate creatures that are present on most deer ranges, only deer predators and livestock will be discussed briefly here.

PREDATORS

Many a verbal battle has raged, and more will occur in the future, over the relationship of deer to their predators and the need for predator control. When the battle lines are drawn, the better-informed sportsmen and land managers and nearly all the biologists and game managers are on one side. The other side usually is made up of professional trappers, some of the older game wardens, and an assortment of sportsmen and ranchers. This group is firm in its belief that heavy control of predators is essential to the abundance and well-being of deer. Biologists and trained wildlife technicians disagree and emphasize the ecological principles involved.

Biologists point out that deer and the animals that prey on deer evolved together. If predators could eliminate their prey, both deer and deer predators would have disappeared millions of years ago. On some ranges in primitive times, wolves and, to a lesser degrees, coyotes running on packed or crusted snow probably caused significant deer losses during severe winters when larger numbers of deer were forced into limited areas. Periodic losses of this kind may have kept the deer populations on such ranges in better balance with their habitats (122a). The influence of the more efficient predators in some places may have limited deer numbers more or less to those that inhabited the more secure habitats (58).

But the fact that deer thrived in primitive times when wolves and

Deer and deer predators evolved together. Even the wolf was unable to check the spread and increase of deer in Canada when deer habitat conditions became right.—*Photo courtesy U.S. Fish and Wildlife Service*

cougars were abundant and subject only to natural controls indicates that less efficient predators, like the bobcat and coyote, cannot exert much influence today. Coyotes, bobcats, and dogs, of course, do kill deer. Occasionally, a pack of coyotes or dogs operating on deep crusted snow may kill significant numbers. Also each spring a number of fawns are killed by coyotes, bobcats, bears, and eagles. In all but the most unusual cases, however, predators take only a fraction of the annual surplus. Often, the prey consists of the weak, the sick, the slow, the less alert, and the less adaptive animals that would be the first to succumb to other factors if there were no predators on the range (58).

A case can be made for the control of free-roaming domestic dogs. On some eastern deer ranges their depredations have been suspected as a limiting factor in the maintenance of optimum deer herds. Unlike native predators, their populations are rarely limited by natural controls, and they can maintain high numbers and efficiency because most are fed and cared for by human owners.

But so long as there is less than a full harvest by hunters of the deer on the range in question, there appears to be no valid reason for the control of coyotes, bobcats, and other wild predators. Only when management becomes so intensive that hunters remove the full surplus of deer each year does the loss of an animal to predators mean one less for the hunter. Under present levels of management, situations of this kind are extremely rare.

There are few instances of intensive predator control leading to substantial increases in deer (123). Even wolves, now practically extinct throughout the United States except in Alaska, have not been able to check the spread and increase of deer in Canada or in those portions of Wisconsin where wolves still exist (172). No recognized deer specialist has reported a case of effective deer control by coyotes (116).

LIVESTOCK

As late as thirty years ago, naturalists claimed that there was little conflict between livestock and deer, because cattle eat grass, sheep eat weeds, and deer feed primarily on browse. This simple mosaic has been shattered by many food habit studies. We know today that all of these animals eat all three kinds of forages.

During the spring months deer feed primarily on grasses and forbs. On many ranges the deer eat these foods wherever and whenever they find them in a succulent growth stage. Cattle, while primarily grass and forb eaters, will supplement their diet with heavy meals of browse whenever the grass supply decreases in nutrient value. Sheep will do the same.

Since colonial times, competition between livestock and deer for forage has been relatively unimportant in the northern forests of New England and the Lake states. In the central hardwood region, livestock use the wild lands to a greater extent, but competition between domestic stock and deer is only locally significant.

In the South, however, as throughout the West, livestock have been and are important competitors with deer, especially on heavily stocked ranges. In Mississippi, on range with only one cow to sixty-three acres, cattle browsed eleven important deer forage species. Researchers estimated that two cows on that range ate as much browse as one deer (92). Goats are serious competitors of deer in Texas. In one investigation, they were found to use twenty-five different deer forage species. Cows on the same area used twelve and sheep only six (16). Hogs also can be troublesome on deer ranges, since they compete with deer for mast. Most investigators, however, concede that the presence of livestock affects deer adversely only where the combined use is so heavy that the deer are forced to take non-preferred foods. Cattle and deer can occupy the same range in relative harmony if both are managed to apply no more than moderate pressure on the key forage species present on their key areas (105).

In Utah, cows tend to occupy the bottoms and lower slopes, while deer are usually found on the middle and upper slopes of the same range (105). Such distribution of deer may be partially a forced situation. Nevertheless, they usually get along well on such common-use ranges where likestock use is not so excessive as to cause food shortages.

Competition between deer and sheep is more direct (163). But, generally, the dietary preferences of the two species allow both to live on the same range in harmony where the sheep stocking is held to a moderate level and the animals are removed from the range during winter (144,163).

A six-year study in Colorado indicated that cattle, sheep, and deer did not compete seriously for forage unless the number of animals was out of balance with the food supply. In this study the researchers compiled lists of choice forage plants by order of their preference for cattle, sheep, and deer. Of the fifteen most preferred by deer, only five appeared on the list for cattle and four on that for sheep. All but one of these browse plants fell into the lower half of the lists for cattle and sheep (144).

Perhaps the most efficient use of some ranges is common use by deer and livestock held at moderate rates of stocking. But at least on

Competition between deer and sheep is more direct than that between deer and cattle, but both can live on the same range without conflict if populations of both are held at moderate levels.—*Photo courtesy U.S. Bureau of Indian Affairs*

the brushier ranges, the native deer is a more efficient feeder than the exotic cow or sheep. On such ranges, deer, in addition to their esthetic and sporting values, produce more meat with less damage to the range than do livestock (35).

Originally, introduction of livestock to the western deer range sometimes benefited and sometimes worked to the detriment of deer. On ranges where cattle and sheep became additional consumers of key food supplies that the deer formerly had for themselves, the impact probably was largely detrimental. On winter ranges, where stable plant associations had flourished for centuries under deer use during the dormant period, the effect of heavy use by livestock must have been especially severe. Livestock use during the spring-fall period left the cupboard bare for the deer when they arrived for the winter, the season when cattle (after 1880) were rounded up and fed (60).

Although no existing records confirm the premise that massive range depletion by livestock caused heavy deer losses, we do know that livestock numbers reached a level where damage to the range became a matter of alarm (60). In the severe winter of 1880-1881, phenomenal livestock losses occurred on much of the western range. Many game animals, faced with depleted food supply, probably also died.

In many situations, however, the long-term effect of livestock grazing was beneficial to deer. The unbroken forests, dense brushlands, and extensive grasslands that blanketed most of North America in primitive times were far from ideal deer habitat.

The relatively stable mixtures of plant species that occupy and dominate broad areas for extensive periods of time under existing climatic and soil conditions are called climax types. Typical climax forests in much of the East consists of a mixture of mature oaks, beech, yellow birch, and other hardwoods. In reaching a climax stage of development, the plant cover passes through several subclimax stages—from grasses and forbs to brushlands, and into and through various successive stages of immature forest. Similar, less dramatic succession takes place in other vegetation types.

Anything that disturbs or destroys the climax vegetation—whether fire, flood, drought, overgrazing, overbrowsing, the plow, axe, bulldozer, or chemical spray—favors invasion by subclimax plants. Repeated disturbance of the cover by any one or a combination of these factors can maintain the subclimax for centuries, as is true of some eastern farmlands. But if climate and soil remain unchanged, the climax species will eventually return and reoccupy the site after the disturbing factor is removed.

Deer usually thrive best where subclimax conditions prevail. Subclimax ranges offer a greater variety of foods and cover types. Neither the ideal livestock range with its broad expanses of unbroken grasslands nor the foresters' dream of mile on mile of mature forest excites the deer-range manager. Some of the most productive deer ranges result from conditions of vegetation that are rated no better than fair and often as poor for livestock or for timber production.

Overgrazing of the western range lands during the dog-eat-dog days of the unregulated open range broke down the climax cover over extensive areas. Subclimax weeds, sagebrush, and other woody plants invaded the denuded lands (117). The chaparral brush types also expanded their ranges (17). It was common practice, according to some range historians, for the stockmen to fire the timber and brush when they left the range in the fall (60). This also tended to favor the establishment and spread of subclimax vegetation.

These changes, and those resulting from logging, land clearing, and temporary mining operations, created what amounted to a new environment for deer. In some places the American deer responded as dramatically as the red deer had in New Zealand, thriving and multiplying in a mighty upsurge of reproduction. In many areas, today, deer are more numerous than they were in primitive times (108, 117, 132, 143).

The more progressive modern stockmen of today know the financial advantage of moderate range stocking. Their emphasis usually is on maximum calf crops and weight and quality of individual animals rather than on numbers alone. Under such practice, competition between domestic and wild animals has been reduced. But there are still ranges where livestock remove so much vegetation that the deer suffer. It is sometimes said there is more competition between deer and other deer than between deer and livestock. Often, this is true, but, on some ranges, livestock still remove the cream of the forage and leave the deer to compete among themselves for what is left.

On the other hand, there are deer ranges that are deteriorating because of insufficient livestock use. This is because heavy grass cover can compete successfully with brush seedlings (17, 68, 96), and prevent the establishment of replacements in a decadent stand of brush plants. On some western ranges used only by deer, grasses are replacing much of the brush. In such situations, regulated use by livestock (or else cultural treatments to discourage grass) may be the most practical method to maintain or improve deer range.

Management techniques designed to favor deer must maintain plant associations that offer a variety of essential deer food and cover types. To return to climax species, with but some exceptions, would be to go out of deer production.

CHAPTER 12

Habitat Management in Brushlands

DEER, LIKE ALL FORMS OF WILDLIFE, NEED SPECIFIC TYPES OF HABITAT to survive. Much of the good deer range that exists over North America today is largely the result of circumstances involving land clearing, logging, livestock grazing, wildfire, homesteading, and other modification of the primitive vegetation cover. Only a minute proportion of this range is managed specifically for deer. If we are to maintain our deer herds at something approaching their present levels, more attention to habitat will be needed in the future. In addition to regulation of hunting, greater emphasis will need be given to habitat management.

In some cases, forests and rangelands can be improved and their carrying capacity for deer increased. Usually this involves altering trends in the plant succession to provide the species and growth stages of vegetation in patterns preferred by deer. In many cases, however, the most that can be done, practically and sensibly, is to maintain conditions that already exist.

Some associations of plants—the sagebrush-bitterbrush type, for example—provide good deer habitat over long periods of time without modification, because their composition and density are relatively stable.

Browseways, like these on the Angeles National Forest in California, open dense brush fields and encourage the growth of browse seedlings, sprouts, and herbaceous forage.—*Photo courtesy U.S. Forest Service*

In such cover types, all that may be needed is the replanting of areas where the desirable forage plants have been destroyed or depleted. There may be need to provide additional sources of water or to provide more cover to shelter deer during adverse weather. Usually, however, the most productive management of such habitat consists of holding deer numbers at optimum levels so as to maintain the productivity of the existing range.

Other types of vegetation, timber or chaparral, must be cut, burned, crushed, or otherwise modified at intervals in order to maintain suitable deer habitat. Once shade and competition for soil space are reduced, a multitude of grasses and forbs develop in the openings. These, along with the sprouts and seedlings of the regenerating brush and trees, provide a varied and rich diet for deer. But as the regenerating plants attain height, their crowns again begin to shade out ground cover and smaller shrubs. The lower limbs of the dominant plants that offer browse to deer die, and the carrying capacity declines.

In such situations deer habitat managers must seek to create new openings or restore the old ones in order to maintain a variety of grasses, forbs, and woody vegetation.

PLANTING BROWSE FOR DEER ON WESTERN RANGE[1]

Many state wildlife agencies have investigated ways to restore browse stands for deer. In fact, in the early fifties, the Western Association of State Fish and Game Commissioners created a Browse Revegetation Committee to review and coordinate such projects in the West. The amount of time and energy devoted to this endeavor should indicate that restoring browse by artificial means is not easy.

Nature, in its extravagance, scatters hundreds of seeds where man can afford to plant only one or two. What percentage of the naturally sown seeds germinate, and what percentage of emergent seedlings survive, no one knows. But we do know that the percentage of survival is infinitesimally low. Man must develop seeding methods much more efficient than those that exist in nature. Planting can be justified, on a broad scale, only if there is a reasonable chance of success.

In the face of the difficulties and high cost of artificial planting, the deer manager must try to husband existing stands and to use all available means to encourage natural propagation. Planting is no cure-all. It should be considered only where natural methods fail.

Planting success is inversely proportional to the amount of other vegetation growing on the site at the time of seed germination. Browse seedlings do not compete readily with grasses, forbs, or established shrubs (96). The best planting success usually is realized where plowing, discing, harrowing, and other regular farming methods are used to prepare a clean, weed-free seed bed. Then, if the rains come at the right time, a high degree of successful germination may take place.

But the problems are not over when the seedlings appear. Drought, frost heave, cutworms, grasshoppers and other insects, rodents, livestock, rabbits, and deer may damage or destroy the young plants. After defending a newly seeded area from a host of potentially destructive agents, the deer manager can appreciate the reason for nature's prodigality in producing and disbursing seed.

Seed Collection. Some species of browse-plant seeds are available from commercial dealers. The commercial supply usually depends on demand. Bitterbrush seed, for example, can be purchased in much of the West for from $1.75 to $3.25 a pound (1970 prices). If there is no supply on the market, seed dealers will often undertake the collection if the

[1]This section draws heavily on material in the *U.S. Forest Service Manual, Region 5 supplement to Section 2632.* I am grateful to the Forest Service for permission to use it.

price and amount desired assure a reasonable profit. If commercial sources fail, it is sometimes possible to interest local individuals and groups in seed collection. Boy Scouts often collect seed for browse plantings made on public lands. However, it may be necessary for the deer manager to collect his own supply of seeds (62).

A light tray with a handle, similar to an oversized dustpan, and a flail are efficient tools for collecting loosely attached seeds. By holding the pan under the bush or tree and flailing the branches above it, the collector catches the seed for sacking. Tightly attached seeds involve more labor and costs. Some of these must be picked by hand, one by one.

Most browse plant seed needs dehulling and cleaning. Field collections usually contain a sizeable proportion of twigs, leaves, and other foreign material. Clean seed is essential to the proper functioning of mechanical planting equipment, and mechanical planting at fixed predetermined depths is the only practical method of assuring success in extensive plantations. Unless one collects seeds in quantities large enough to warrant the cost of purchasing a seed cleaner, it will be necessary to send the field-collected seed to a commercial plant for dehulling and cleaning (62).

Preparing the Seed Bed. In establishing a browse plantation, site selection, site preparation, and soil moisture are the most important factors. The most dependable sites are those known to have supported the same

Seed collection for small-scale habitat improvement can be done with simple equipment, but large-scale operations require the use of more sophisticated machinery, like this vacuum seed picker.—*Photo courtesy U.S. Forest Service*

plant species in the past (95). If the site is new, or if its past history is uncertain, its soil and climatic characteristics should be compared carefully with those of areas supporting stands of the same species. If the comparison is favorable, site preparation is the next step.

Planting may be done on cleared or formerly cultivated areas or in natural clearings. Regular farming equipment may be used to prepare a seed bed on the larger sites. The work involves plowing or discing and drilling in the seeds. If the drill is not equipped with a metering device to space the seeds, good results can be obtained by mixing rice hulls with the seed in a ratio governed by seed size. Eight pounds of rice hulls to three pounds of seed works well for bitterbrush. Enough of the seeding tubes should be blocked to provide four-foot spacing between the rows. Depth of planting varies with the species, and with soil types. For bitterbrush it varies from a little less than one inch in heavy soils to a little more than an inch in light soils. Bitterbrush usually is planted at the rate of three pounds to the acre (62).

Ordinarily, browse seeds should be planted in the fall to permit dormancy breakdown during the winter. Where soil moisture is marginal and adequate rainfall not dependable, it may be necessary to withhold planting until the spring of a favorable year. When this is done, the seed will have to be treated to break down dormancy, either through regular stratification methods or by immersion in thiourea or other chemicals. Thiourea quickly breaks the dormancy of such seeds as bitterbrush (95, 97). Treated seed must be planted as soon as the site is dry enough to support equipment. The soil should be firm enough and contain enough moisture to establish a good union with the seed. Press wheels should be used on the drill where they are available because they help pack the soil around the seed (62).

Spot planting may be used on areas too small or otherwise unsuited for heavy equipment. This consists of hoeing off the existing vegetation for at least three feet around the planting spots. A planting tool similar to a common corn planter works well. It may be used efficiently on steep slopes and in rocky areas that are inaccessible to mechanized equipment (62).

Browse establishment has no shortcuts. Failures often occur when the best methods are faithfully applied. Requirements, of course, vary by regions and sites. More exacting site preparations and soil treatments are needed on some areas than on others. As precipitation and other factors favorable to germination improve, difficulties in establishing stands of browse on wild lands usually decrease and this may allow changes in technique. In Idaho, for example, bitterbrush planting realized considerable success where the seeding was done with a flexiplanter—a combination of plow, seeder, and press wheel. In the longleaf pine belt of Texas, satisfactory stands of yaupon were established in cut-over clearings with no treatment other than removal of all woody plants (111).

Attempts to establish browse plantings in the face of heavy browsing pressure are rarely successful. A study in Wisconsin showed that deer were crippling 600 million tree seedlings and young trees in the state each year. Planting from 40 to 60 million seedlings a year did little to solve the problem (167). Attempts to improve the quality and quantity of browse in Pennsylvania also failed because of an overabundance of deer (114).

Often, when deer numbers are reduced to a point where moderate cropping of forage prevails, nature will do a better job of revegetating ranges than can be expected from artificial planting. On the other hand, where the better forage species are scarce or absent, the expense of establishing plantations may be necessary and justified.

GRASS PLANTINGS

Grassy openings are important to deer. They provide edge vegetation and add variety to the diet. Grasslands can be established in forest or brush ranges by a number of methods: The most successful is a formula consisting of the following steps: cutting or crushing, burning, planting, and spraying.

Grass plantings, like those of browse, are most successful where regular farming methods can be used to reduce competition from existing vegetation. Thousands of tons of good grass seeds have been wasted through lackadaisical site preparation and planting methods. The use of agricultural or rangeland drills to plant seeds in measured quantities at fixed depths usually pays off in improved germination and plant survival.

Where wildfire sweeps deer range, herbaceous vegetation should be planted before it rains to help hold the soil as well as to provide forage. Broadcast seeding in the ash often provides a good plant cover under such situations. In the West, annual grasses are more easily established at lower elevations. Elsewhere, perennial grasses and legumes should be used.

MODIFYING CHAPARRAL BRUSH RANGE

The low shrubby forest known as chaparral has developed partly in response to climate and soil conditions and partly through the influence

In areas accessible to machinery, drills like this are the most practical means of establishing deer food plants. This deep-furrow drill plants both bitterbrush and crested wheatgrass.—*Photo courtesy U.S. Forest Service*

of the wildfires which have burned this inflammable vegetation over the centuries (102). All the principal component species of chapparral are either vigorous crown-sprouters or produce heat-resistant and heat-germinating seed. Deer relish the regenerating vegetation that follows a burn in chaparral. For a year or two after a fire, they eagerly seek out the shoots of shrubs that, in their mature state, are low on the palatability scale.

Controlled burning is a common and relatively inexpensive method of improving chaparral range for deer. Periodic burning creates a temporary profusion of sprouts, seedlings, and herbaceous vegetation that is far more nutritious than the mature brush. The increase in the amount of available vegetation as a result of controlled fire in the chaparral is dramatic. A California study found that overmature brush stands yielded from 13 to 106 pounds of available deer browse per acre, depending upon the brush type. After a crush-and-burn treatment the same or comparable areas yielded around 800 pounds of browse per acre of lands burned in the previous autumn and up to 1800 pounds per acre on those burned in early spring (68). Areas crushed by tractor prior to burning give the deer greater accessibility to the large varieties of palatable foods produced by the controlled burn. A crush-burn deer habitat improvement project on the west slope of the Sierra Nevada in California resulted in an increase of use from 100 to 172 deer days per acre (44a).

Early efforts to reduce the density of brush by burning followed by heavy browsing by domestic sheep were unsuccessful (142). More recently investigators have found that the number of sprouts and seedlings can be reduced by a combination of burning, grass establishment, and heavy browsing followed by a second burning (11). Chemical brush control can be substituted for the second burn where it is safer from the standpoint of soil erosion or other values.

Nonsprouting chaparral species usually can be reduced by two burns, preferably two years apart (142). The establishment of herbaceous cover on a burn of this kind has several benefits. Grasses slow the invasion of brush, stabilize the soil, and provide forage for range animals. They also build up fuel for a second burn where this is needed (11).

The objective of chaparral brush management is to open the stands by spot burning or mechanical clearing to create interspersion of food and cover. The initial size of each opening should be relatively small and the total area treated restricted to allow moderate browsing by deer. The hedging of the regenerating brush by deer creates and maintains an open formation of shrubs interspersed with herbaceous cover. Untreated brush cover should be left in patches of forty acres or more. At maximum development, about one-third of the original cover on

The object of habitat improvement in chaparral is to break up the solid stands of brush with grassy openings.—*Photo courtesy U.S. Forest Service*

south slopes and two-thirds on north slopes should be left undisturbed. On managed shrublands of this kind, deer increased both in numbers and productivity (169).

When brush ranges are managed intensively, deer numbers may build up to a level where browsing pressure kills or weakens the preferred browse species. Where deer can maintain satisfactory numbers on a diet consisting of the more common chaparral and herbaceous plants, the loss of preferred browse species may be of small importance. On the other hand, if, as is true elsewhere, preferred species are found necessary to provide essential dietary needs, a decline of these forage plants will affect the deer populations adversely.

Obviously, each stand of shrubland has characteristics of its own, and management plans must be altered accordingly. It is important to keep records of changes in deer densities and plant communities at different stages of development. Special attention should be given to less abundant preferred forage species. Basic information of this kind proves invaluable in detecting vegetation changes and their effects on deer.

Chemical brush killers have become a useful tool for eliminating or reducing the density of undesirable brush species. The use of such sprays usually is more economical and practical in some vegetation types than is burning or mechanical clearing. These compounds are particularly useful in areas where fire hazards are high. Spraying to kill brush, followed by later burning to remove the dead material at a safer season, is effective when the immediate use of fire would be dangerous or where the brush is too green to burn. Of course, only approved chemicals that do not have damaging or cumulative effects on the environment should be used.

With some browse species, such as birch-leaf mahogany, crushing alone may be the best treatment. It is particularly useful on deer concentration areas where seedlings need protection (68).

The sprouting species of brush are more difficult to control than are nonsprouters, and they require more intensive treatment. Because of this, an inventory of the stand is essential before plans for manipulation are complete.

Finally, as a word of caution, fire should be used to improve deer range only by people expert in its use and in conformity with all local and state laws. Loosed by the inexperienced or overoptimistic, it can be a destroyer and killer.

Browseways for Hungry Deer. Browseways are lanes crushed through stands of dense brush, usually of tractor-blade width. The bulldozer is the most commonly used implement, but sometimes these lanes are created by hand. The heavy-duty roto-beater or similar flailing instrument is capable of cutting or crushing brush to within a foot of the ground.

Browseways facilitate access both by deer and man. The rejuvenating brush sprouts and seedlings also offer a rich supply of forage that is higher in succulence and nutrients than the adjoining untreated brush.

The browseway system of habitat management is used widely on the national forests of southern California. The lanes do not disturb vegetation or soil to a degree that causes significant accelerated soil erosion. They offer a safe means for extensive treatment of brushlands in regions of high fire hazard, since they create little dry fuel or the need for slash burning.

There are three types of browseways:

1) The extensive browseway usually consists of one or two parallel lanes established along ridgetops in mountainous areas with steep slopes and unstable soils.

2) The checkerboard browseway, practical on flats or gentle slopes, consists of a crisscross pattern of intersecting lanes which creates blocks or islands of undisturbed cover, regulated in size by the intensity of management desired.

3) The contour browseway, as its name implies, consists of parallel lanes established along contour lines on moderate slopes on which soil movements could become a problem.

Browseways established in California brushlands remain useful to deer for from ten to twenty years in stands well stocked with palatable browse species. Moderate browsing tends to hedge back the plants in the lanes and hold them in an available form. The total area treated should not be so large as to distribute the browsing pressure too thinly. It is best to widen the clearings on flats, benches, and swales, in order to develop a walkway and island pattern. So long as the overall area treated is not too large for the existing deer population to handle, the islands will provide a higher acreage of palatable browse less affected by the spread of the untreated shrubs along the edges.

The average cost of construction in California of 2860 acres of browseways was $30 per acre. It was found on the Cleveland National Forest in that state that use of browseways by deer was about nine times heavier than in nearby untreated brush, averaging 34 deer days per acre. Browseways on that national forest were still functioning fourteen years after construction (44a).

CHAPTER 13

Deer Habitat Management in Forests

DENSE FORESTS MAKE POOR DEER HABITAT. WE ALREADY HAVE SEEN that mature coniferous forests on the West Coast often support no more than two deer to the square mile (31). This is true of dense stands of timber everywhere. This general low deer density and lack of productivity result from the monopoly of sunlight and soil nutrients by the established trees. The herbaceous or shrubby vegetation that does establish itself in the half-shade along watercourses or in the scattered small openings usually is deficient in protein (55).

The value of timberland for deer is proportional to the degree that it is broken and interspersed with openings (174). Deer numbers on forested lands usually are highest where openings that support low-growing palatable shrubs and herbs are scattered through the forest. Some of these openings may be natural meadows, marshes, or areas with soils that favor grasses and shrubs at the expense of trees. Other openings may be created by logging, wildfire, or farm abandonment. In some places, wildlife managers are creating similar openings where needed to improve habitat for deer.

Aspen stands can be managed to provide an abundance of deer browse. The tops of these felled trees provide an immediate source of food. An abundance of suckers and stump sprouts will assure a food supply next winter.—*Photo courtesy Ontario Department of Lands and Forests*

DEER AND FORESTRY

In the old days, the forests were exploited without thought of the future. In the East, the virgin hardwood and coniferous forests were logged, burned, cleared, homesteaded, grazed, and subjected to repeated wildfire. With farm abandonment and more particularly with fire protection, the land was reclothed gradually with maple, birch, aspen, oak, and other hardwood species, interspersed with clumps and thickets of conifers and dotted with openings supporting herbaceous vegetation—an ideal deer habitat. Where present, the deer thrived and multiplied.

Today much of the eastern forests are reaching a stage of height and density that will no longer support the deer populations of a few years ago. The process has been accelerated by extensive conifer planting by foresters of clearings and natural openings.

In the West, the cutout-burnout-and-getout logging created huge brush fields supporting manzanita, oaks, wild lilacs, mountain mahogany, serviceberry, and other shrubs. Many of these brushfields remain today with little or no timber cover. The western cut-over lands, especially when adjacent to water, supported and some still support high populations of deer—a product of poor silvicultural practice.

But in the face of mounting land and other resource values, the wasteful forest exploitation that created this excellent deer habitat is not apt to be repeated. The brushfields are being reclaimed by type conversions of shrubs to conifers. Even where wildfires destroy large acreages of timber today, many foresters now plant trees at once, rather than wait for the slow process of natural reforestation. As a result, the deer habitat in the western forests is declining.

Modern logging, whether it involves block cutting or selective group cutting, does provide an interspersion of openings that benefit deer. But with the advent of sustained-yield forestry and more efficient silviculture, the carrying capacity of the forests for deer has been much reduced below that of the wasteful past.

Logically, the first priority in the management of timberlands—especially those in private ownership—is to grow trees. Foresters usually welcome deer on such lands, so long as they do not interfere with this objective. One important phase of modern forestry is the rapid reforestation of logged areas. The aim is to get the tree seedlings established before other kinds of vegetation can move in and dominate the site. Once the young trees are established, the invasion of shrubs, grasses, and forbs is of little concern to the forester. In from ten to thirty years, the new stand of trees will reach full density and shade out the lower vegetation. Hence, the span of time that forest plantations remain useful to deer is relatively short.

Most of the benefits to deer that occur from normal forestry operations are accidental or incidental. In most situations, there is a need to modify management if forests are to be managed for high deer production. In the North, where heavy coniferous cover is so important to deer in winter, saving groups of trees of the proper age and density in yarding locations can be essential. In areas where cover is abundant and food is scarce, a system of rotated clearcuts, thinning and sanitation cuts will provide a variety of plants in different age classes. Cuttings of this kind can increase the browse supply up to forty-five times over that present in mature forests. Even thinnings can produce fourteen times more browse than that available in uncut stands (57).

The use of abandoned farmland and other forest openings as sites for pine plantations works to the detriment of deer and many other forms of forest wildlife. The conversion of mixed pine-hardwood forest to stands of pure pine by girdling, cutting, or chemical treatments now being carried out extensively in the South and elsewhere, has a similar effect. These practices have reduced the hardwood browse and mast or fruit essential to wildlife. If, in spite of the teachings of ecology and the adverse experience with single-species stands in Europe, these forestry practices are continued and become more general, we may look for a further serious decline in deer abundance in many states.

In an effort to offset part of the damage associated with pine culture, Texas researchers established yaupon in longleaf pine forests. Four years after planting the yaupon growing in clearings averaged fifty inches in height, and one-third of the plants bore fruit. The plants growing under pines averaged seventeen inches in height and bore no fruit. Plants on cleared areas produced fifty-seven times as much vegetation as those under pines—a clear indication of the importance of clearings in deer management (111).

Over much of the East the year-long range of a group of deer may consist of 2000 acres or less. The quality of such individual ranges may be maintained by a series of properly spaced and timed clearcuts. Cutting about one-quarter of the area, approximately 500 acres, every twenty years, will provide good balance between young and old timber stands. The former produce browse, the latter cover and mast (156).

The current trend toward intensive even-aged forest management has caused concern among deer managers. This concern has generated a great deal of research which has led to prescriptions that may be applied in cooperative programs between foresters and wildlife managers.

For instance, in Wisconsin it is thought that northern mixed hardwood-conifer forest can produce sustained yields of both timber and deer if 5 percent of the land is left in permanent openings. Here, it is recommended that all openings of less than five acres in size be left unplanted, that sod-covered openings be maintained within well-populated summer range, and that no attempt be made to control invading woody plants by herbicidal treatments so long as deer browsing is heavy enough to retard the establishment of tree seedlings (124a).

In northern Minnesota, where aspen covers nearly one-third of the commercial forest land, natural succession is converting many aspen stands to spruce or fir—species of much less value for deer. Aspen is a fast-growing tree that attains full growth in forty to fifty years. It begins to deteriorate after sixty years and is commonly replaced by conifers. When aspen is cut, it regenerates rapidly from root suckers and stump sprouts, and for the first few years provides abundant food for deer. The Minnesota Department of Conservation recommends the maintenance of aspen on medium to good growing sites by the cutting of both merchantable and nonmerchantable trees on a fifty-year rotation basis. The cutting should be done on numerous small and well-distributed spots each year, giving special priority to areas adjacent to deer yards. The conversion of aspen to conifers by plantings should be limited to poor aspen growing sites (150a).

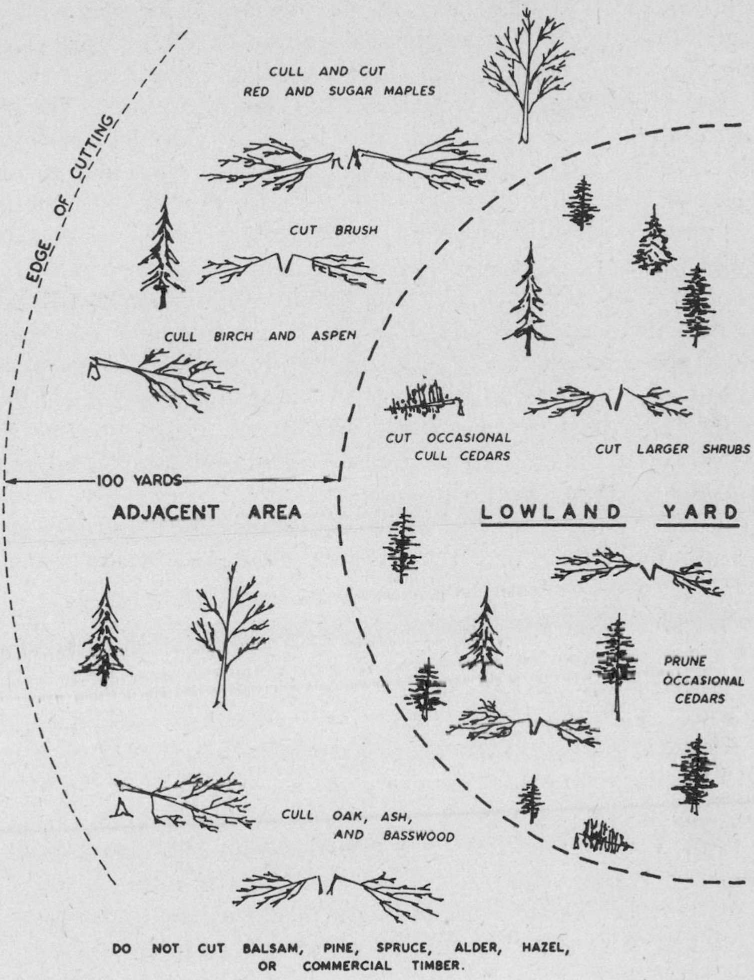

Improvement of Lowland Deer Yards with White Cedar or Balsam Cover

The Minnesota Department of Conservation recommends winter cutting of browse as shown in diagram.—*Reproduced from* A Minnesota Guide to Forest Game Management *by LeRoy H. Rutske, courtesy Division of Game, Minnesota Department of Conservation*

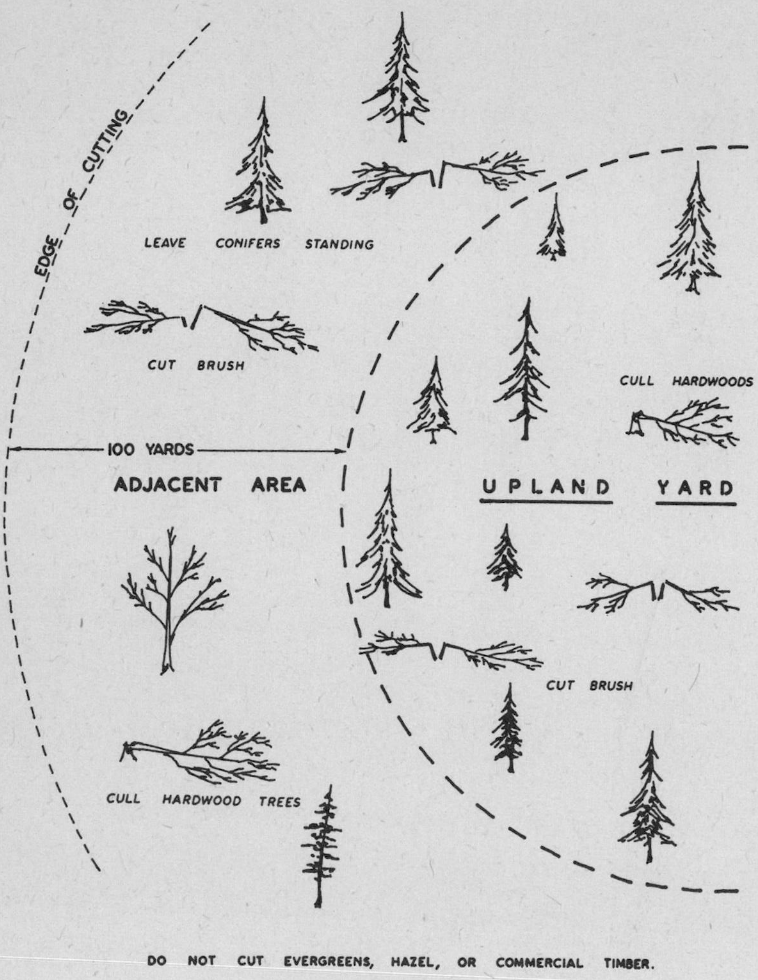

Improvement of Upland Deer Yards of Balsam, Spruce, or Pine

Diagram shows procedure of winter cutting browse recommended by the Minnesota Department of Conservation.—*Reproduced from* A Minnesota Guide to Forest Game Management *by LeRoy H. Rutske, courtesy Division of Game, Minnesota Department of Conservation*

At the present time, a comparatively low demand for pulpwood in relation to available supply, makes it difficult to maintain aspen stands through commercial cutting operations. Only 1 percent of the forested land in Minnesota is being logged each year—a cutting cycle of 100 years. Under such conditions, it may become necessary to make additional cuttings primarily to preserve aspen and benefit deer. Fortunately, both foresters and wildlife managers agree it would be beneficial for the pulpwood industry as well as for deer to reduce the rotation period by one-half (127a).

Minnesota wildlife specialists also recommend that all existing small forest openings be preserved and that additional small openings be created by cultural methods. Where larger openings are planted, they recommend that conifer plantings be made in three- to five-acre blocks separated by open strips at least sixty-five feet wide and surrounded by an unplanted perimeter of the same width (150a).

We have already discussed the importance of dense cover for deer in winter in northern climes. In both Minnesota and Maine, spruce-fir stands are more frequently used as winter yarding areas than are those of northern white cedar. Such stands of large trees can be improved as deer yarding areas by clearing a series of alternate narrow strips or checkerboard blocks no more than two chains wide to provide

A number of northern paper and pulpwood companies maintain and improve deer yards in cooperation with state wildlife agencies.—*Photo courtesy Maine Fish and Game Department*

shrubby browse adjacent to the winter cover. Where uneven-aged management of spruce-fir swamps is desirable from a silvicultural standpoint, selective cutting should be planned so as to maintain at least 50 percent crown closure in order to provide winter shelter for deer (150a).

In Missouri, the Department of Conservation and the U.S. Forest Service have embarked on a cooperative forest game habitat management program on public forests with a goal of providing range for not fewer than 8 turkeys, 31 deer, and 300 squirrels on each 1000 acres. These populations are considered "acceptable" from the standpoint of hardwood forest management.

The Missouri forests are typical of much of the hardwood region. Here, the recommendations to meet the wildlife goals provide for the establishment of at least one reliable source of water per square mile and the preservation of all existing openings up to 5 percent of each management unit. Sharecropping, grazing, periodic controlled burning, mowing, or tilling are used to maintain these openings. The cooperative recommendation also calls for the restoration of former openings that have been planted to pines by commercial clear-cutting at the earliest possible date (46a).

In many of the industrialized states, power lines and other utility rights-of-way provide permanent artificial openings or strips of low cover that are heavily used by deer and other wildlife. Missouri's cooperative program suggests that the utility companies, under the terms of easement agreements, maintain these areas in productive condition by selective clearing and other maintenance (46a).

In Missouri, as elsewhere, there is a strong trend toward even-age forest management. In order to preserve the silvicultural advantages of even-aged management and the diversity of cover needed by wildlife, Missouri manages its commercial forests on a compartment basis. The cooperative program recommends that at least 10 percent and not more than 20 percent of each compartment be regenerated to oak or pine during each ten-year period in order to achieve a balance of age-size classes. The composition of age-size classes includes 40 percent of the acreage in sawtimber, 30 percent in poles, 20 percent in saplings, and 10 percent in seedlings. Because of the importance of acorns in the diet of deer and other forest wildlife, at least 45 percent of the forest stand on each unit will be maintained in a mast-producing condition, with at least one-third of the acorn-producing trees in the white oak group (46a).

In their cooperative program, Missouri's wildlife specialists found themselves in conflict with foresters only on minor points. Their principal point of disagreement was on size of management areas. Foresters preferred units of several thousand acres while wildlife managers wanted areas not larger than 1000 acres, in order to achieve a more even interspersion of age-size classes within the ranges of the deer and other forest wildlife species. Similar prescriptions have been developed by wildlife specialists for use in providing benefits for deer in timberland throughout the nation.

DEER DAMAGE IN FORESTS

There is a place for deer in the managed forest, but it is a regulated and shifting place. Deer aggregations drift from cutting to cutting in the wake of the logger, following and governed by the cutting cycle. If trees and deer are to be raised on the same land, the deer population must be maintained at a level that will minimize economic damage.

Under modern intensive forestry, fear of economic damage to trees by deer nags the forest industry. Investments in tree plantation often run as high as $100 or more per acre, and the prospect of losing ten or twenty years of production to deer is not a reassuring one.

Fortunately, there are indications that native trees tolerate a moderate amount of browsing without serious damage. On a study area in British Columbia, for example, young Douglas fir trees in plantations managed to grow out of reach of the deer despite repeated setbacks resulting from browsing of their tips or leaders. Moderate browsing during the first five years after planting did not seriously retard their long-term rate of growth or have a permanent effect on the form of the tree. At twelve years of age, browsed trees averaged forty inches in height compared to sixty inches for unbrowsed trees. The British Columbia study indicated that Douglas fir plantations can support deer without serious damage so long as numbers of animals are kept within reasonable limits (129). Again, a thirty-year study in Louisiana revealed that shortleaf and loblolly pine trees browsed by rabbits within an inch or two of the ground the year they were planted equalled in most instances, and sometimes exceeded, unbrowsed trees in survival, diameter, dominance, and height growth. Rabbit-browsed slash pine did not do so well as unbrowsed, but did better than trees of the same species planted one year later (177a). Chances are that the effect of first-year deer browsing does not differ greatly from that of rabbits. However, on heavily browsed forest ranges in California, a comparable study found that annual height growth of Douglas fir seedlings averaged only 2.7 inches as compared with 8 inches for young trees protected from deer browsing. Once conifers attained a height of from three to four feet, they were able to escape deer browsing, but it was found here that it required 13 to 18 years for the suppressed trees to reach that height (15). Whether the deer-suppressed trees were later able to catch up in height and form with the protected trees is still to be determined.

In assessing deer damage to forest stands, the important thing is not the number of trees that are heavily browsed but the number that escape serious damage. Foresters normally plant around 500 tree seedlings to the acre with the ultimate objective of cutting 80 mature trees. While adequate density and close spacing of young trees encourages height growth and development of proper form, most tree plantations contain many more trees than are needed. So long as the deer leave enough lightly browsed or undamaged trees to develop an adequate mature stand, little or no harm is done.

Deer researchers in Massachusetts surveyed the browsing pressure on young hardwoods in deer sanctuaries and in other places where deer were protected. They found that browsing heavy enough to suppress trees permanently ranged up to around 30 percent of the young trees present. Even under the level of heaviest use, however, the deer left undamaged an average of 269 stems per acre, more than enough to insure forest growth on the areas under consideration (154).

Michigan, Wisconsin, Pennsylvania, and other eastern states where deer numbers have been permitted to grow out of balance with their food supplies have sometimes suffered particularly acute damage to their forests (114, 167). The adoption of antlerless deer seasons, especially where deer are managed on the management unit basis, has done much to correct such problems.

Most publicly owned forest lands, particularly those within the national forests, are managed, theoretically at least, under the concept of multiple use. Timber, watersheds, livestock, recreation, and wildlife supposedly receive equal emphasis. In a few key places the production of deer and other forest wildlife has received priority over that of saw-logs and pulpwood. On some public forests where conservation interest is high, permanent openings are maintained to enhance the wildlife habitat.

In the main, however, the principal concern of forest management has been to grow trees. If the wildlife manager and the sportsman wish to develop a broader and more cooperative attitude among foresters, they will have to support the regulation of deer populations at levels that can be carried without serious conflict with silviculture. Conversely, foresters charged with the responsibility of managing our public lands must deliberately seek to create greater public benefits on the lands that they administer.

On many forested deer ranges there are opportunities to improve deer habitat by cultural methods. But, ordinarily, the most practical way to improve and maintain deer habitat is to regulate the numbers of animals that use it. Even on ranges where cultural methods substantially increase the forage supply, deer populations must be held at levels where their demand for food does not exceed the enhanced supply. Otherwise, the full productivity of the deer herd and its range cannot be maintained.

FARMLAND DEER RANGE

Within the past fifty years or less white-tailed deer have re-invaded farmlands from central New England to Florida in the East and in much of the Middle West in response to improved habitat conditions and protection. Much of this heterogeneous range now supports healthy deer herds.

The better farm deer range in the East is characterized by comparatively small land-holdings under a wide variety of uses—cropfields, pasture, woodlot, and orchard—all often occurring on the same farm. Many farms are separated by woodlands of various sizes and in various degrees of management ranging from well-tailored conifer plantations to neglected forests that have regenerated on abandoned land.

Except in the extreme northern portion of this farmland deer range, whitetails seldom yard except in the most severe winters and food and water are usually both abundant and well-distributed.

The diversity of the land-use pattern in eastern farming country makes specific management recommendations difficult. But the future of the deer on these lands will depend largely upon the maintenance of the woodlots, shrubby hedgerows, and wooded bottomlands that now provide them with browse, escape cover, and travel lanes.

CHAPTER 14

Fundamentals of Deer Management

THE KINDS OF PALATABLE PLANTS THAT OCCUR ON DEER RANGES TODAY have survived the assaults of deer through the ages because they have developed resistance to browsing. All are characterized either by tolerance to pruning, rapid growth, cagelike or thorny branch patterns that protect interior foliage, or some other adaptation that permits their survival. Thus, by one means or another, enough of the native forage plants have withstood the ravages of high deer populations to perpetuate their species over broad regions even though occasionally heavy deer browsing may have eliminated the more palatable plants from limited areas.

There are natural checks on the growth of any deer population once it increases above the optimum carrying capacity of its range. These natural population controls help prevent complete depletion of forage plants. But from a human standpoint, they are far from ideal, because they result in waste.

When deer increase beyond the numbers that their range will support in good health, the animals suffer. Every fawn that survives under such conditions adds to the problem. Eventually, a population level is reached where one deer must die before there is room for another. The number of animals that survives each year is the maximum the habitat will support during the season of shortest supply.

Habitat shortages, particularly food deficiencies, reduce fawn production and fawn survival. They cause a decline in weight, size, and physical condition of the adult animals. They reduce the antler development in bucks, and they increase day-to-day losses to diseases, parasites, accidents, and outright starvation.

Excessive browsing of forage plants accelerates the waste of animals. As the plants lose vigor, they produce less growth. The lowered production of twigs and leaves further reduces a food supply already inadequate to meet the demand.

This pushes the deer herd closer to the brink of disaster. A drought, a hard winter, or an outbreak of disease can cause heavy losses. Then, for a while, deer will be scarce.

Such recurring periods of deer scarcity bring relief to the range. The surviving forage plants respond to their release from heavy browsing. Gradually, they recover vigor, produce more abundant growth, accumulate reserves of food, and scatter seed crops. New plants become established. Older plants push up branches and tops above the reach of deer or develop densities that protect interior growth. The productivity of the range goes into an upswing.

The period of deer scarcity after such a die-off varies in duration with the nature of the range. On transitory range like that in eastern forests, deer may not repopulate the area until the next cut or burn. On stable range, like some the brushlands of the West, the period of deer scarcity may be much shorter. But when the proper stage is set, the animals will multiply. Thus the cycle of abundance to scarcity, scarcity to abundance is repeated again and again.

One of the principal objectives of deer management is to hold the number of animals on each range at a level in balance with the supply of nutritious forage, potable water, and adequate cover. When this objective is achieved, the deer maintain high levels of health and productivity, and the wide fluctuations in their number are reduced.

Nothing in nature is static, including the maximum carrying capacity of a deer range. The population ceiling of a unit will rise during good years and fall during poor years. Many die-offs of deer result from such fluctuations. The herd will build up during a succession of favorable years to a population level much higher than the normal ceiling, only to face severe readjustment when changing conditions result in a rapid drop in carrying capacity. During such readjustment periods, severe range damage may, and often does, occur.

Apart from its recreational value, hunting benefits both the deer and the deer range.—*Photo courtesy U.S. Forest Service*

The only way to maintain balance between deer and the habitat is to remove the surplus animals each year. In the United States this is best accomplished by regulated hunting seasons. Apart from the economic returns—including those realized by merchants, outfitters, guides, rural resorts, and small-town businesses—hunting benefits both the deer herd and deer range by removing animals that otherwise would be lost and wasted.

If a population of deer is managed so as to reduce the number of animals in the herd each year to a more or less fixed level that is below the maximum carrying capacity of the range, it will result in a sustained yield. The percentage of the population that may be taken by hunters under sustained-yield management will vary with the intensity of management applied. A high percentage of animals can be taken from a population reduced annually to a low level at which both production and survival of fawns is high. Or a low percentage of animals can be taken from a high-level population whose fawn production and survival are low. The optimum (in terms of numbers rather than percentage) will lie somewhere between the two (59a).

A deer herd, for instance, may be managed for a sustained yield of trophy bucks. This will result in a low percentage yield from a high population. Or it may be managed for a sustained yield of deer of either sex, which may result in a sustained yield approaching the optimum. On units where there is a high intensity of hunting, use of dogs, and poor distribution of escape cover, either-sex hunting may result in a high percentage yield from a low population. In most situations, the objective in management should be to harvest the optimum sustained yield of deer.

Removing part of the buck population each year leaves the remaining animals with a somewhat enhanced share of the things they need. Fawn production and winter survival usually are better under buck hunting than they are in unhunted herds (122). But with buck hunting alone, the yield of deer falls far short of the potential, and the does are left to fill out the range. Because deer are polygamous, buck hunting has little effect on the rate of increase of the herd. It removes only a fraction of the number of deer that would ordinarily die each year because of shortages of one kind or another.

Either-sex deer hunting permits an annual harvest up to its full potential—one-quarter to one-third of the animals present before the hunting season. When surplus animals are removed, the controls exerted by habitat shortages slacken. The taking of a sizable number of deer of both sexes each fall permits the survival of a larger proportion of those that otherwise would have perished. And because the survivors have a larger share of nutritious food and the other things they need, breeding success is enhanced and there is a larger production of young. So long as each year's crop of surplus animals is removed each autumn, this productive situation continues.

Once a deer population has been brought into balance with its

In spite of excellent examples like this hardwood-recycling cutting in Ontario, the possibilities for deer habitat improvement have only been scratched.—*Photo courtesy Ontario Department of Lands and Forests*

habitat, the only way to increase the number of healthy deer is to expand or improve the habitat. With mounting land values and increasingly intensive land use, opportunities for expanding the forests and brushlands that make up America's deer range are limited. But much of the existing deer range can be improved. In some places it may be necessary to improve the quality or quantity of forage plants; in others the need may be to develop shelter for deer during adverse weather, to create openings in extensive stands of dense forests, or to develop reliable water supplies and so open up many square miles of dry range to use by deer.

Opportunities for deer habitat improvement seem much more promising under present and foreseeable future conditions than those for habitat expansion. The Forest Service administers over 180 million acres of federal land. Under its multiple-use concept, the Forest Service has recognized the importance and value of deer habitat management for many years. In many eastern states, federal foresters work closely with state wildlife biologists to develop timber cutting programs on national forests that help protect winter deer yards, enhance food and cover conditions, and encourage hunter access to areas with overpopulations of deer. In the West, key winter deer ranges on national forests are usually given special protection and in some cases have been improved by plantings and other cultural treatment. In Virginia, the Game and Inland Fisheries Commission requires any hunter using the two national forests in the state to purchase a special-use stamp, the revenues of which are applied to wildlife habitat improvements on the federal lands.

In recent years the Bureau of Land Management, which administers nearly 500 million acres of public lands in the western states and Alaska—much of it outstanding deer range—belatedly has moved into the arena of federal-state cooperative wildlife management. There is agreement among wildlife professionals that much more can and must be done on the national forests and the public domain to improve conditions for our invaluable fish and wildlife resources.

In the private sector, similar outstanding examples of cooperation between the state agencies and the forest products industries exist. Several of the timber and pulp companies holding large blocks of lands in northern New England have standing agreements with the state wildlife agencies to protect critically important deer yards. Comparable arrangements exist on the industrial and privately owned tree farms of the Northwest, the Lake States, and the South.

In spite of these encouraging examples, the possibilities for habitat improvement for deer have only been scratched. As the demand for recreational hunting increases, much more intensive management of the existing deer range will be required.

Under well-established principles of law, ownership of wildlife is vested in the state. The official wildlife agency, by whatever name it may be known in each state, is the custodian of the deer and all other resident wildlife.

Custodianship of any public resource implies responsibility for its management. The establishment of hunting regulations is one manifestation of that responsibility. Hunting is the most practical method of maintaining deer populations in balance with their habitat, of protecting other forest and range resources from damage by deer, of preventing excessive agriculture crop depredation, of minimizing motor vehicle accidents involving deer, and of maintaining a healthy and vigorous deer population.

In each state today the official wildlife agency employs biologists trained to appraise the age composition of the deer herd, the trend in deer numbers, the physical condition and productivity of the individual animals, the condition of the deer range, and other factors on which sound hunting regulations may be based.

Too frequently, these carefully made recommendations are blocked from implementation by public or political pressure stemming from misguided sentimentality or from fear that relaxed hunting regulations will drastically reduce or even will exterminate the deer. Such fears are poorly founded. The objective of deer management in this time of increasing demand for sport and esthetic enjoyment is to produce the maximum crop of healthy animals each season consistent with other uses of the land.

Since deer range is dynamic, changing with fluctuations in weather and food supply and shifting animal-use patterns and pressures, no rate of deer stocking may be considered final on any individual range. Adjustments must be made in response to changing conditions. The majority of the states today employ various forms of zoning, and they vary the hunting regulations for each zone in accordance with prevailing range condition, deer population, and hunting pressure.

Fortunately, nearly all states today have departed from inflexible hide-bound adherence to the buck law and similar long-entrenched holdovers from the dark ages of wildlife management. Either-sex and antlerless-deer hunting seasons have become the rule rather than the exception. Progress of this kind, although slow in coming, is a welcome sign that America's sportsmen and the public at large have reached maturity in their attitudes toward ecological problems, including the need for managing deer.

Information Kit

COMMON AND SCIENTIFIC NAMES OF DEER

Common	Scientific
California mule deer	*Odocoileus hemionus californicas*
Columbian black-tailed deer	*Odocoileus hemionus columbianas*
Desert mule deer	*Odocoileus hemionus eremicus*
Inyo mule deer	*Odocoileus hemionus inyoensis*
Red deer	*Cervus elaphus*
Rocky Mountail mule deer	*Odocoileus hemionus hemionus*
Southern mule deer	*Odocoileus hemionus fuliginatus*
White-tailed deer	*Odocoileus virginianus*

COMMON AND SCIENTIFIC NAMES OF PLANTS WESTERN PLANTS

Alfalfa	*Medicago sativa*
Aspen	*Populus tremuloides*
Bearberry	*Arctostaphylos uvi-ursa*

Big sagebrush	*Artemesia tridentata*
Birch-leaf mahogany	*Cercocarpus betuloides*
Bitterbrush	*Purshia tridentata*
Black sagebrush	*Artemesia tridentata nova*
Black oak	*Quercus kelloggii*
Bluegrass	*Poa* spp.
Blue oak	*Quercus douglasii*
Bluebunch wheatgrass	*Agropyron spicatum*
Buckbrush	*Ceanothus cuneatus*
Bud sagebrush	*Artemesia spinescens*
California bay	*Aesculus californica*
California black oak	*Quercus kelloggii*
California redberry	*Rhamnus crocea*
Canyon live oak	*Quercus chrysolepsis*
Ceanothus	*Ceanothus*
Chamise	*Adenostoma faciculatum*
Chaparral pea	*Pickeringia mustana*
Chokecherry	*Prunus virginiana demissa*
Cliff rose	*Cowania stansburiana*
Clover	*Trifolium* spp.
Curl-leaf mahogany	*Cercocarpus ledifolius*
Dandelion	*Taraxacum* spp.
Desert saltgrass	*Distichlis stricta*
Douglas fir	*Pseudotsuga taxifolia*
Elderberry	*Sambucus* spp.
Fir	*Abies* spp.
Gambel oak	*Quercus gambelii*
Hollyleaf cherry	*Prunus illicifolia*
Honeysuckle	*Lonicera* spp.
Idaho fescue	*Festuca idahoensis*
Indian ricegrass	*Oryzopsis hymenoides*
Interior live oak	*Quercus wizlizenii*
Junegrass	*Koelaria cristata*
Juniper (Colorado)	*Juniperus scopulorum*
Lupine	*Lupinus* spp.
Maple	*Acer* spp.
Mountain white oak	*Quercus garryana*
Oregon grape	*Berberis* spp.
Oregon oak	*Quercus garryana*
Pine	*Pinus* spp.
Poison oak	*Rhus diversilova*
Pentstemon	*Pentstemon*
Rabbitbrush	*Chrysothamnus* sp.
Red juniper	*Juniperus virginiana*
Red osier	*Cornus stolonifera*
Redstem	*Ceanothus sanguineus*
Redwood	*Sequoia sempervirens*
Sagebrush	*Artemesia* spp.
Scrub oak (California)	*Quercus dumosa*
Scrub oak (Colorado)	*Quercus gambelii*

Serviceberry (western)	*Amelanchier alnifolia*
Silktassel	*Garrya* spp.
Silver sagebrush	*Artemesia cana*
Snowberry	*Symphoricarpos* spp.
Snowbrush	*Ceanothus velutinus*
Soft chess	*Bromis mollis*
Spruce	*Picea* spp.
Squaw carpet	*Ceanothus prostratus*
Squirreltail	*Sitanion hystrix*
Staghorn sumac	*Rhus glabra*
Tobacco brush	*Ceanothus velutinus*
Turbinella oak	*Quercus turbinella*
Utah juniper	*Juniperus utahensis*
Valley white oak	*Quercus lobata*
Water oak	*Quercus lobata*
Western hemlock	*Tsuga heterophylla*
Western red cedar	*Thuja plicata*
Wild grape	*Vitis* spp.
Wild lilac	*Ceanothus* spp.
Wild rose	*Rosa* spp.
Yellow pine	*Pinus ponderosa*

EASTERN PLANTS

Acacia	*Acacia* spp.
Alternate dogwood	*Corvus alternifolia*
Apple	*Pyrus* sp.
Balsam	*Abies balsamifera*
Beautyberry	*Callicarpa americana*
Blackberry	*Rubus* sp.
Black cherry	*Prunus serotina*
Black haw	*Viburnum rubidulum*
Blackjack oak	*Quercus marilandica*
Black oak	*Quercus nigra*
Black titi	*Cliftonia monophylla*
Blueberry	*Caccinium* spp.
Dog hobble	*Viburnum alnifolium*
Eastern red cedar	*Juniperus virginiana*
Flowering dogwood	*Cornus florida*
Forestiera	*Forestiera* sp.
Greenbrier	*Smilax rotundifolia* and other spp.
Hackberry	*Celtis* spp.
Hazel	*Corylus* spp.
Hemlock	*Tsuga canadensis*
Jack pine	*Pinus banksiana*
Laurel-leaf	*Smilax laurifolia*
Live oak	*Quercus virginia*
Loblolly pine	*Pinus taeda*
Longleaf pine	*Pinus australis*
Maple	*Acer* spp.

Mountain ash	*Pyrus americana*
Mountain laurel	*Kalmia latifolia*
Mountain maple	*Acer spicatum*
Northern white cedar	*Thuja occidentalis*
Pasture juniper	*Juniperus communis*
Persimmon, Texas	*Diosyros texana*
Plum	*Prunus americana*
Post oak	*Quercus stellata*
Pussytoe	*Antennaria* spp.
Red bay	*Persea borbonia*
Red maple	*Acer rubra*
Redstem	*Ceanothus sanguineus*
Sassafras	*Sassafras albidum*
Shinoak	*Quercus undulata mohriana*
Shortleaf pine	*Pinus echinata*
Smooth hydrangea	*Hydrangea arvorescens*
Sourwood	*Oxydendrum arboreum*
Sumac	*Rhus* spp.
Sweetleaf	*Symplocos tinctoria*
Tulip poplar	*Liriodendron tulipifera*
Tupelo gum	*Nyssa aquatica*
Water oak	*Quercus nigra*
Wax myrtle	*Myrica pacifica*
White ash	*Fraxinus americana*
White oak	*Quercus alba*
White titi	*Cyrilla racemiflora*
Wild grape	*Vitis canadensis*
Willow oak	*Quercus phellus*
Yaupon	*Ilex vomitoria*
Yellow birch	*Betula*
Yellow jessamine	*Gelsemium sempervirens*
Yellow pine	*Pinus ponderosa*
Yew	*Taxus candensis*

MONTHLY VARIATION IN PERCENTAGE OF CRUDE PROTEIN IN WESTERN PLANTS

Species	J	F	M	A	M	J	J	A	S	O	N	D
					Grasses							
California melic‡	24	—	19	11	4	3	—	—	—	—	—	—
Slender wildoats‡	21	17	8	7	4	2	—	2	2	—	—	22
Soft chess‡	—	23	20	14	8	6	—	5	4	—	—	—
					Forbs							
Late valley lupine‡	—	32	27	23	12	5	—	—	—	—	—	28
Whitestem filaree‡	27	—	15	9	4	—	—	—	—	—	—	—
					Browse Species							
Big sagebrush*	10	10	9	12	9	—	11	10	—	11	10	10
Bitterbrush*	7	7	7	10	11	—	—	11	—	9	10	8
Blue oak‡	—	—	19	12	13	14	—	—	11	—	—	—
Buckeye*	—	—	26	31	—	21	20	11	11	5	—	—
Bush lupine‡	16	—	24	24	17	13	—	—	12	—	13	—
California redberry*	8	—	—	—	16	10	—	11	7	8	—	—
Chamise*	6	8	11	14	14	10	9	6	6	4	7	7
Chaparral whitethorn‡	—	13	15	17	14	12	—	—	9	10	—	—
Desert mahogany*	7	6	6	7	9	—	8	12	—	—	8	9
Fourwing saltbush†	—	6	—	6	22	18	15	12	10	—	8	—
Fremont silktassel*	8	8	9	12	10	10	7	5	6	6	6	6
Interior live oak*	9	9	8	18	18	11	10	10	7	7	8	8
Poison oak*	—	—	24	23	21	16	10	10	7	4	—	—
Scrub oak*	8	9	10	14	15	12	11	7	7	6	9	7
Wavyleaf ceanothus*	8	10	13	17	25	11	9	7	8	7	8	8
Wedgeleaf ceanothus‡	—	13	17	12	11	10	—	—	7	—	11	—
Western mahogany*	7	7	14	17	15	12	12	9	8	8	10	9
Yerba santa*	8	10	10	17	12	9	5	7	6	7	7	7

*Data adapted from Bissell, Harold D. and Helen Strong. 1955. The crude protein variations in the browse diet of California deer. *California Fish & Game* 41(2): 145-156.

†Data adapted from Costello, David F. 1944. Post-war thinking for the cattle breeder. Rocky Mountain Forest and Range Experiment Station.

‡Data adapted from Gordon, Aaron and Arthur W. Sampson. 1939. Composition of common foothill plants as a factor in range management. *University of California Experiment Station Bulletin* No. 627. 95 pp.

PERCENTAGES OF CRUDE PROTEIN IN SOUTHERN BROWSE PLANTS*

Species	Spring	Winter
Beautyberry	18	8†
	22	11‡
Black gum	13	3
Buckwheat tree	12	5
Common buttonbush	14	—
Common sweetleaf	17	8†
	20	9‡
Elder	18	—
Flowering dogwood	—	5-7
Greenbrier	—	11
Red bay	16	7
Red maple	—	3-6
Rose bay rhododendron	—	4
Sweet bay		10
Sweet pepperbush	13	—
Virginia sweetspire	21	11
White oak	—	7
Yaupon	9	7†
	15	11‡
Yellow jessamine	—	8

*Halls, Lowell K. and Thomas H. Ripley. 1961. Deer browse plants of southern forests. Forest Service, U.S.D.A., and Wildlife Society (Southeastern Section). 78 pp.
†Unburned.
‡Burned.

References

1 Adams, Lowell
1949 The effects of deer on conifer reproduction in northwestern Montana. *Journal of Forestry* 47(11):909-913.

2 Aldous, C. M.
1945 A winter study of mule deer in Nevada. *Journal of Wildlife Management* 9(2):145-151.

3 Aldous, Shaler E.
1941 Deer management suggestions for northern white cedar types. *Journal of Wildlife Management* 5(1):90-94.

4 Anon.
1937 The best deer food. *Michigan Conservation Bulletin* 6(11):2 (Hosley, 1956).

5 Ashcraft, Gordon C.
1961 Deer movements of the McCloud Flats herd. *California Fish & Game* 47(3):145-152.

6 Bartlett, I. H.
1950 *Michigan Deer.* Michigan Game Division. 50 pp.

8 Bissell, H. D., B. Harris, H. Strong and F. James
1955 The digestibility of certain natural and artificial foods eaten by deer in California. *California Fish & Game* 41(1):57-78.

9 Bissell, Harold D. and Helen Strong
1955 The crude protein variations in the browse diet of California deer. *California Fish & Game* 41(2):145-156.

10 Bissell, Harold D.
1959 Interpreting chemical analysis of browse. *California Fish & Game* 45(1):57-58.

10a Bissell, Harold
1969 Personal communication.

11 Biswell, H. H., R. D. Taber, D. W. Hedrick and A. M. Schultz
1952 Management of chamise brushlands for game in the north coast region of California. *California Fish & Game* 38(4):543-484.

12 Brody, S., R. C. Proctor and V. S. Ashworth
1934 *Growth and development with special reference to domestic animals.* Missouri Agricultural Experiment Station. Research Bulletin No. 220.

13 Bromfield, Louis
1949 Poor land makes poor hunting and fishing. *Field & Stream,* January issue.

14 Brown, Ellsworth Reade
1959 *The black-tailed deer of Western Washington.* Washington State Game Department Biological Bulletin No. 13. 124 pp.

15 Browning, Bruce M. and Earl M. Lauppe
1964 A deer study in the Redwood-Douglas-fir forest type. *California Fish & Game* 50(3):132-147.

16 Buechner, Helmet Karl
1944 The range vegetation of Kern County, Texas, in relation to livestock and white-tailed deer. *American Midland Naturalist* 31(3):697-743.

17 California Division of Forestry
1960 *The brush problem on California livestock ranges.* California Division of Forestry. 30 pp.

18 Carhart, Arthur H.
1945 What Deer Eat. *The American Field* 143(2):28-29.
1946 *Hunting North American Deer.* Macmillan. 232 pp.

19 Chapline, W. R. and M. W. Talbot
1926 *The use of salt in range management.* U.S.D.A. Department Circular No. 379.

20 Cheatum, E. L. and C. W. Severinghaus
1950 Variations in fertility of white-tailed deer related to range condition. 15th Transactions North American Wildlife Conference: 170-189.

21 Cook, C. W., L. A. Stoddard and L. E. Harris
1951 Measuring consumption and digestibility of winter range plants by sheep. *Journal of Range Management* 4(5):335-346.

23 Cowan, Ian McTaggart
1945 The ecological relationships of the food of the Columbian black-tailed deer in the coast forest region of southern Vancouver Island, British Columbia. Ecological Monographs (15):109-139.

24 Cowan, Ian McTaggart
1950 Some vital statistics of big game on over-stocked mountain range. 15th Transactions North American Wildlife Conference: 581-588. North American Wildlife Conference.

25 Cowan, Ian McTaggart and A. J. Wood
1955 The growth rate of the black-tailed deer. *Journal of Wildlife Management* 19(3):331-336.

26 Cowan, Ian McTaggart
1956 Life and times of the coast black-tailed deer. *Deer of North America.* Stackpole.

27 Cowan, R. L. and T. A. Long
1962 Studies of antler growth and nutrition of white-tailed deer. Proceedings National White-tailed Deer Disease Symposium 1:54-60.

28 Dahlberg, Burton L. and Ralph C. Guettinger
1956 *The white-tailed deer in Michigan.* Wisconsin Conservation Department. Technical Bulletin No. 14. 282 pp.

29 Dalke, Paul D.
1941 The use and availability of the more common winter deer browse plants in the Missouri Ozarks. 6th Transactions North American Wildlife Conference: pp. 155-160.

31 Dasmann, Raymond F. and William H. Hines
1959 Logging, plant succession, and black-tailed deer in the redwood region. Humboldt State College, Arcata, Calif. 12 pp. (Mimeo).

32 Dasmann, Raymond F.
1962 Conservation by slaughter. *Pacific Discovery* 15(2):3-9.

33 Dasmann, Raymond F. and William P. Dasmann
1963 Mule deer in relation to a climatic gradient. *Journal of Wildlife Management* 27(2):196-202.

34 Dasmann, Raymond F.
1963 *The last horizon.* Macmillan, 279 pp.

35 Dasmann, Raymond F.
1964 Biomass, yield and economic value of wild and domestic ungulates. Proceedings of Union of International Game Biologists. Bournemouth, England.

37 Dasmann, William P.
1948 A critical review of range survey methods and their application to deer range management. *California Fish & Game* 34(4):189-207.

38 Dasmann, William P.
1950 Can we hold the western range. *Pacific Discovery* 3(4):17-23.

39 Dunkeson, Robert L.
1955 Deer range appraisal for the Missouri Ozarks. *Journal of Wildlife Management* 19(3):358-364.

41 Dasmann, William P.
1952 The deer range. California Department of Fish and Game Deer Management Handbook. 37 pp. (Mimeo).

42 Dasmann, William P. and James A. Blaisdell
1954 Deer and forage relationships on the Lassen-Washoe interstate deer range. *California Fish & Game* 40(3):215-232.

43 Dasmann, William P. and Henry A. Hjersman
1958 Deer survival and range forage trends on eastern California winter ranges. *California Fish & Game* 44(1):51-72.

44 Dasmann, William P. and Raymond F. Dasmann
1963 Abundance and scarcity in California Deer. *California Fish & Game* 49(1):4-15.

44a Dasmann, W., R. Hubbard, W. G. MacGregor and A. E. Smith
1967 Evaluation of wildlife results from fuelbreaks, browseways, and type conversions. Proceedings California Tall Timbers Ecology Conference: 179-193.

45 Davis, Richard B.
1948-49 Food habits and population studies of white-tailed deer on the live oak-mesquite ranges of the King ranch. *Texas Cooperative Wildlife Research Unit Quarterly Report* 9(4):2-6 (Hosley, 1956).

46 Day, Benjamin W., Jr.
1964 *The white-tailed deer in Vermont.* Vermont Fish and Game Service. 24 pp.

46a Dellinger, George P.
1970 Habitat management for turkeys in the oak-hickory forests of Missouri. Proceedings of the Second National Wild Turkey Symposium, Feb. 11-12. University of Missouri Press.

47 Deming, Oscar V.
1959 Climate, range and antelope. Transactions of the Interstate Antelope Conference. 27 pp.

48 Dietz, D. R., R. U. Udall and L. E. Yeager
1962 Chemical composition and digestibility by mule deer of selected forage species, Cache La Poudre Range, Colorado. Colorado Fish and Game Department Technical Bulletin No. 14. 89 pp.

50 Dixon, Joseph
1934 A study of the life history and food habits of mule deer in California. *California Fish & Game* 20(3-4). 146 pp.

51 Doman, Everett R. and D. I. Rasmussen
1944 Supplemental feeding of mule deer in northern Utah. *Journal of Wildlife Management* 8(4):317-338.

52 Donaldson, David, Carl Hunter and T. H. Holder
1951 *Arkansas Deer Herd.* Arkansas Game annd Fish Commission. 72 pp.

53 Downs, Albert A. and William E. McQuilken
1944 Seed production of southern Appalachian oaks. *Journal of Forestry* 42(12):913-920 (Hosley, 1956).

55 Einarsen, Arthur S.
1946 Crude protein determination of deer food as an applied management technique. 11th Transactions North American Wildlife Conference: 309-312.

57 English, P. F. and W. C. Bramble
1949 Kill 'em!—Starve 'em!—Feed 'em! Deer eat the best forage they can find. Pennsylvania State College, School of Agriculture Experiment Station, 61st Annual Report, Bulletin 502, Supp. 3:7-8 (Hosley, 1956).

58 Errington, Paul L.
1946 Predation and vertebrate populations. *The Quarterly Review of Biology* 21(2):144-177.

59 Ferrel, Carol M. and Howard Leach
1952 Deer food habit studies. California Department of Fish and Game. (Unpublished).

59a Food and Agriculture Organization of the United Nations
1970 *Wildlife investigation techniques handbook.* In press.

60 Forest Service
1936 *The Western range.* U.S. Government Printing Office. 620 pp.

61 Forest Service
1937 *Range plant handbook.* U.S. Government Printing Office.

62 Forest Service
1963 *Forest Service Manual,* Title 2600. Region 5 Supplement to FSM 2632.4. (Mimeo).

63 Forsling, C. L. and E. V. Storm
1929 *The utilization of browse forage on summer range for cattle in southeastern Utah.* U.S.D.A. Circular 62. 29 pp.

64 French, C. E., L. C. McEwen, N. D. Magruder, R. H. Ingram and R. W. Swift
1955 *Nutritional requirements of white-tailed deer for growth and antler development.* Pennsylvania State University Agriculture Extension Service Bulletin 600. 50 pp.

65 Garrett, W. N.
1963 Shade for beef cattle. University of California, *Successful Farming,* August 1963.

66 Gerstell, Richard
1937 Winter deer losses. *Pennsylvania Game News* 8(7):18-21 (Hosley, 1956).

67 Gerstell, Richard
1938 The Pennsylvania deer problem in 1938. *Pennsylvania Game News* 9(5):12-13, 31; 9(6):10-11, 27, 38; and 9(7):6-7, 29 (Hosley, 1956).

68 Gibbens, R. P. and A. M. Schultz
1963 Brush manipulation on a winter deer range. *California Fish & Game* 49(2):95-118.

68a Giles, Robert H. and Ted McKinney
1968 Feeding deer to death. *National Wildlife* 6(1):46-47.

69 Gill, John D.
1957 *Review of deer yard management.* Maine Department of Inland Fisheries and Game. Game Bulletin No. 5. 61 pp.

70 Goodrum, Phil D. and Vincent H. Reid
1958 Deer browsing in the longleaf pine belt. 1958 Proceedings, Society of American Foresters, pp. 139-143.

71 Gordon, Aaron and Arthur W. Sampson
1939 *Composition of common California foothill plants as a factor in range management.* University of California Agricultural Experiment Station Bulletin No. 627. 95 pp.

72 Grasse, James E.
1949 The 1949 white-tail transplant. *Wyoming Wildlife* 13(2):2-9. (Hosley, 1956).

73 Green, Lisle E., L. A. Sharp, C. W. Cook and L. E. Harris
1951 Utilization of winter range forage by sheep. *Journal of Range Management* 4(4):233-241.

74 Gruell, G.
1958 Results from four years of trapping and tagging deer in northeastern Nevada. Proceedings Western Association of State Game and Fish Commissioners 38:179-183.

75 Gruell, George E. and Nick J. Papez
1963 Movements of mule deer in northeastern Nevada. *Journal of Wildlife Management* 27(3):414-422.

76 Guilbert, H. R. and G. H. Hart
1946 *California beef production.* California Agricultural Experiment Station Bulletin No. 131. 155 pp.

77 Gwynn, Jack V.
1965 Deer management: quality or quantity, *Virginia Wildlife* 26(1).

78 Hagen, Herbert L.
1953 Nutritive value for deer of some forage plants in the Sierra Nevada. *California Fish & Game* 39(2):163-176.

79 Hahn, Henry G.
1945 *The white-tailed deer in the Edwards Plateau region of Texas.* Texas Game and Fish Commission F.A. Report No. 2. 52 pp.

80 Halls, Lowell K. and Thomas H. Ripley
1961 *Deer browse plants of southern forests.* Forest Service, U.S.D.A. 78 pp.

81 Hamerstrom, F. N. and James Blake
1939 Winter movements and winter foods of white-tailed deer in central Wisconsin. *Journal of Mammalogy* 20(2):206-215.

82 Harris, D.
1945 Symptoms of malnutrition in deer. *Journal of Wildlife Management* 9(4) 319-322.

83 Hart, George H.
1952 Livestock diet utilization. *California Agriculture,* February issue.

84 Hart, George H.
1952 The importance of management in livestock operations. *California Cattlemen,* February issue.

86 Hayes, Doris W. and George A. Garrison
1960 *Key to woody plants of eastern Oregon and Washington.* U.S.D.A. Agricultural Handbook No. 148. 227 pp.

86a Hayes, H. H., N. F. Colovos and H. Silver
1964 Therapeutic value of soil for enteritis in white-tailed fawns. New Hampshire Fish and Game Department.

87 Heady, Harold F.
1963 Management of grazing resources in the redwood region. University of California. 7 pp. (Mimeo).

88 Hellmers, Henry
1940 A study of monthly variations in the nutritive value of several natural winter deer foods. *Journal of Wildlife Management* 4(3): 315-325.

89 Herman, Carlton K.
1945 Deer management problems as related to disease and parasites of domestic range livestock. 10th Transactions North American Wildlife Conference: 242-246.

90 Hormay, August L.
1943 Bitterbrush in California. California Forest and Range Experiment Station Research Note No. 34. 13 pp.

91 Howard, Walter E.
1964 Introduced browsing animals and habitat stability in New Zealand. *Journal of Wildlife Management* 28(3):421-429.

92 Hosley, Neil W.
1956 Management of the white-tailed deer in its environment. *The deer of North America.* Stackpole, pp. 187-260.

93 Hosley, N. W. and R. K. Ziebarth
1935 Some winter relations of white-tailed deer to the forests in north central Massachusetts. *Ecology* 16(4):535-553.

95 Hubbard, R. L., E. C. Nord and L. L. Brown
1959 Bitterbrush seeding, a tool for the range manager. Pacific Southwest Forest and Range Experiment Station Miscellaneous Paper No. 39. 14 pp.

96 Hubbard, R. L. and H. R. Sanderson
1961 Grass reduces bitterbrush production. *California Fish & Game* 47(4):391-498.

97 Hubbard, R. L. and H. R. Sanderson
1961 When to plant bitterbrush—spring or fall? Pacific Southwest Forest and Range Experiment Station Technical Paper No. 64. 21 pp.

98 Humbert, John and William Dasmann
1945 Range management—a restatement of definitions and objectives. *Journal of Forestry* 43(4):263-264.

99 Hunter, Gilbert N. and Lee E. Yeager
1949 Big game management in Colorado. *Journal of Wildlife Management* 13(4):392-411.

100 Interstate Deer Herd Committee
1951 The Devils Garden deer herd. *California Fish & Game* 37(3):233-272.

101 Jensen, Wallace and W. Leslie Robinette
1955 A high reproductive rate for Rocky Mountain mule deer. *Journal of Wildlife Management* 19(4):503.

102 Jepson, W. L.
1925 *A manual of flowering plants in California.* University of California Press. 1238 pp.

102a Joint FAO/WHO Expert Group
1965 Protein requirements. WHO Technical Report Series No. 301; FAO of U.N., Rome. 71 pp.

103 Julander, Odell
1937 Utilization of browse by wildlife. Second Transactions of North American Wildlife Conference: 276-287.

104 Julander, Odell and W. Leslie Robinette
1951 Deer, harvest or starve them. *Utah Fish & Game Bulletin,* May issue.

105 Julander, Odell
1955 Deer and cattle range relations in Utah. *Forest Science* 1(2):130-139.

106 Julander, Odell, W. Leslie Robinette and Dale A. Jones
1961 Relationship of summer range condition to mule deer herd productivity. *Journal of Wildlife Management* 25(1):54-60.

107 Krefting, L. W., M. H. Stenlund and R. K. Seemel
1966 Effect of simulated and natural browsing on mountain maple. *Journal of Wildlife Management* 30(3):481-488.

108 Lang, E. M.
1957 *Deer in New Mexico.* New Mexico Department of Fish and Game. Bulletin No. 5. 41 pp.

109 Lassen, Robert W., Carol M. Ferrel and Howard Leach
1952 Food habits, productivity and condition of the Doyle deer herd. *California Fish & Game* 38(2):211-224.

110 Latham, Roger M.
1950 Pennsylvania's deer problem. *Pennsylvania State News,* Special Issue No. 1. 48 pp.

111 Lay, Daniel W.
1966 Forest clearings for browse and fruit plants. *Journal of Forestry* 64(10):680-683.

112 Leach, Howard
1956 Food habits of the Great Basin deer herds in California. *California Fish & Game* 42(4):243-308.

113 Leach, Howard and Jack L. Hiehle
1957 Food habits of the Tehama deer herd. *California Fish & Game* 43(3):161-178.

114 Leffler, Ross L.
1948 Our deer problem and its effect on the management of food and cover for wildlife. 38th Proceedings International Association of Fish, Game and Oysters Commissioners.

115 Leopold, Aldo
1933 *Game management.* Scribner, 481 pp.

116 Leopold, Aldo, L. K. Sowls and D. L. Spencer
1947 A survey of over-populated deer ranges in the U.S. *Journal of Wildlife Management* 11(2):162-177.

117 Leopold, A. Starker
1950 Deer in relation to plant succession. 13th Transactions North American Wildlife Conference. pp. 571-580.

118 Leopold, A. Starker, T. Riney, R. McCain and L. Tevis
1951 *The Jawbone deer herd.* California Department of Fish and Game. Game Bulletin No. 4. 139 pp.

119 Lindner, A. M., M. Brandl and E. Wyler
1956 New methods to prevent game damage. *Allgemeine Forstzeitung,* Vienna (67):233-237.

120 Linsdale, J. and P. Q. Tomich
1953 *A herd of mule deer.* University of California Press, Berkeley, California. 567 pp.

121 Lommasson, T. and Chandler Jensen
1942 *Determining the utilization of range grasses from height-weight tables.* U.S. Forest Service, Northern Region. 9 pp.

122 Longhurst, William M., A. S. Leopold and R. F. Dasmann
1952 *Survey of California deer herds, their ranges and management problems.* California Department of Fish and Game Bulletin No. 6. 136 pp.

122a Lovaas, Allan L.
1970 *People and the Gallatin elk herd.* Montana Fish and Game Department, Helena. 44 pp.

123 Madson, John and Edward Kozicky
1961 A closer look at predation. *Wildlife Review* 8(2).

124 Maynard, L. A., G. Bump, R. Darrow and J. C. Woodward
1935 *Food preferences and requirements of white-tailed deer in New York State.* New York Conservation Department Bulletin No. 1. 35 pp.

124a McCaffrey, Keith R. and William A. Creed
1969 *Significance of forest opening to deer in northern Wisconsin.* Technical Bulletin No. 44. Wisconsin Department of Natural Resources.

126 McGinnies, W. G., K. W. Parker and G. E. Glendening
1941 Southwestern range ecology. U.S. Forest Service, Region 3. 211 pp. (Mimeo).

127 Meyer, James H.
1952 Letter to author. University of California at Davis.

127a Minnesota Department of Conservation
1969 A deer management program for Minnesota. Division of Game and Fish. 11 pp. (Mimeo).

128 Mitchell, H. L. and N. W. Hosley
1936 Differential browsing by deer on plots variously fertilized. *Black Rock Forest Papers* 1(2):24-27. (Hosley, 1956).

129 Mitchell, K. J.
1964 Height growth losses due to animal feeding in Douglas-fir plantations, Vancouver Island, B.C. *Forestry Chronicle* 40(3):298-307.

130 Morton, James N. and John B. Sedam
1938 Cutting operations to improve wildlife environment on forest areas. *Journal of Wildlife Management* 2(4):206-214.

131 Murie, Claus J.
1951 *The elk of North America.* Wildlife Management Institute. Stackpole. 376 pp.

132 Nevada Legislative Counsel Bureau
1959 *Survey of fish and game problems in Nevada.* Bulletin No. 6. 160 pp.

133 Nichol, A. A.
1938 *Experimental feeding of deer.* University of Arizona Technical Bulletin No. 75. 39 pp.

134 Olson, H. F.
1938 Deer tagging and population studies in Minnesota. 3rd Transactions North American Wildlife Conference. pp. 280-286.

135 Olsen, Orange A.
1945 Relationship of big game and livestock on Western ranges. *Elk Below:* 53-65. Privately published.

136 Ozoga, John L. and Elsworth M. Marger
1966 Winter activities and feeding habits of northern Michigan coyotes. *Journal of Wildlife Management* 30(4):809-818.

139 Pearce, John
1937 The effect of deer browsing on certain western Adirondack forest types. *Roosevelt Wildlife Bulletin* 7(1):1-61. (Hosley, 1956).

139a Pimlott, D. H.
1967 Wolf predation and ungulate populations. *American Zoology* 7:267-278.

140 Rasmussen, D. I. and Everett R. Doman
1943 Census methods and their application in the management of mule deer. 8th Transactions North American Wildlife Conference: 369-379.

141 Ratcliff, Harold M.
1941 Winter range conditions in Rocky Mountain National Park. 6th Transactions North American Wildlife Conference: 132-139.

142 Reynolds, H. G. and Arthur D. Sampson
1943 Chapparal crown sprouts as browse for deer. *Journal of Wildlife Management* 7(1):119-122.

143 Reynolds, Temple A.
1960 *The mule deer, its history, life history, and management in Utah.* Utah Department of Fish and Game. Information Bulletin No. 60-4. 32 pp.

144 Riordan, Laurence E.
1958 Some results of a ten-year study of deer-livestock competition for range forage. Colorado Fish and Game Department. 14 pp. (Mimeo).

145 Robinette, W. Leslie
1966 Mule deer home range and dispersal in Utah. *Journal of Wildlife Management* 30(2):335-349.

146 Robinson, Cyril S.
1937 Plants eaten by California mule deer on the Los Padres national forest. *Journal of Forestry* 35(8):285-292.

147 Robinson, D. J.
1956 Preliminary studies upon the effect of logged-over areas on quality and size of deer populations on Vancouver Island. British Columbia Game Commission. 5 pp. (Mimeo).

149 Rosen, M., O. A. Brunetti, A. I. Bischoff and J. A. Azevedo
1951 An epizootic of foot-rot in California deer. 16th Transactions North American Wildlife Conference: pp. 164-168.

150 Ruff, Frederick J.
1938 The white-tailed deer on the Pisgah national game preserve, North Carolina. Forest Service. 249 pp. (Mimeo) (Hosley, 1956).

150a Rutske, LeRoy H.
1969 *A Minnesota guide to forest game habitat improvement.* Minnesota Division of Game and Fish.

151 Sampson, Arthur W. and Beryl S. Jespersen
1963 *California brushlands and browse plants.* California Agricultural Experiment Station Manual 33: 162 pp.

152 Schilling, E. A.
1938 Management of white-tailed deer on the Pisgah national game preserve. 3rd Transactions North American Wildlife Conference: pp. 248-255. (Hosley, 1956).

153 Severinghaus, C. W.
1953 Springtime in New York, another angle. *New York State Conservationist* 7(5):2-4.

154 Shaw, S. P. and C. L. McLaughlin
1951 *The deer in Massachusetts.* Division of Fisheries and Game Research Bulletin No. 13: 59 pp.

155 Shaw, Samuel P.
1951 The effect of insufficient harvests on an Island deer herd. Proceedings Northeastern Fish and Wildlife Conference.

156 Shaw, Samuel P. and Thomas H. Ripley
1965 Managing the forest for sustained yield of woody browse for deer. 1966 Proceedings, Society of American Foresters: pp. 229-233.

157 Smith, Arthur D.
1949 Effects of mule deer and livestock upon a foot-hill range in northern Utah. *Journal of Wildlife Management* 13(4):421-423.

158 Smith, Arthur D.
1950 Feeding deer on browse species during winter. *Journal of Range Management* 3(2):130-132.

159 Smith, Arthur D.
1950 Differential consumption of juniper by mule deer. *Utah Fish and Game Bulletin* 9(5).

160 Smith, Arthur D.
1950 Sagebrush as a winter feed for mule deer. *Journal of Wildlife Management* 14(3):285-289.

162 Smith, Justin G.
1952 Food habits of mule deer in Utah. *Journal of Wildlife Management* 16(2):148-155.

163 Smith, Arthur D. and Odell Julander
1953 Deer and sheep competition in Utah. *Journal of Wildlife Management* 17(2):101-112.

164 Stoddard, L. A. and D. I. Rasmussen
1945 Big game-range livestock competition on western ranges. 10th Transactions North American Wildlife Conference: 251-256.

165 Swank, Wendell G.
1958 *The mule deer in Arizona chapparal.* Arizona Game and Fish Department. Wildlife Bulletin No. 3. 109 pp.

166 Swift, Ernest
1946 *A history of Wisconsin deer.* Wisconsin Conservation Department Publication 323. 96 pp.

167 Swift, Ernest
1948 Deer damage to forest reproduction survey. 38th Proceedings International Association of Fish, Game and Oyster Commissioners.

168 Symington, D. F. and W. A. Benson
—— *White-tailed deer in Saskatchewan.* Saskatchewan Department of Natural Resources Conservation Bulletin No. 2. 17 pp.

169 Taber, Richard D. and Raymond F. Dasmann
1958 *The black-tailed deer of the chaparral.* California Department of Fish and Game. Game Bulletin No. 8. 163 pp.

171 Taylor, Walter P.
1947 Some new techniques—hooved animals. 12th Transactions North American Wildlife Conference: pp. 293-324.

172 Thompson, Daniel Q.
1952 Travel, range and food habits of timber wolves in Wisconsin. *Journal of Mammalogy* 33(4):429-442.

173 Thomas, J. W., J. G. Teer and E. A. Walker
1964 Mobility and home range of white-tailed deer on the Edwards Plateau in Texas. *Journal of Wildlife Management* 28(3):463-473.

174 Titus, Harold
—— *Timber and game—twin crops.* American Forest Products Industries. 33 pp.

175 Trippensee, R. W.
1948 *Wildlife management.* McGraw-Hill, New York. 479 pp.

176 Van Volkenburg, H. L. and A. J. Nicholson
1943 Parasitism and malnutrition of deer in Texas. *Journal of Wildlife Management* 7(2):220-223 (Hosley, 1956).

177 Verme, Louis J.
1963 Effect of nutrition on growth of white-tailed deer fawns. 28th Transactions North American Wildlife Conference: pp. 431-443.

177a Wakeley, Philip C.
1970 Long-time effects of damage by rabbits to newly planted southern pines. *Tree Planters Notes.* U.S.D.A. Forest Service. 21(2):6-9.

179 White, K. L.
1960 Differential range use by mule deer in the spruce-fir zone. *Northwest Science* 34(4):118-126.

181 Young, Vernon A. and Gene F. Payne
1948 Utilization of "key" browse species in relation to proper grazing practices in cutover western pine stands in northern Idaho. *Journal of Forestry* 46(1):35-40 (Hosley, 1956).

182 Zalunardo, Raymond A.
1965 Movements of a mule deer herd. *Journal of Wildlife Management* 29(2):345-351.

183 Zwickel, F., G. Jones and H. Brent
1953 Movement of Columbian black-tailed deer in the Willipa Hills area, Washington. *Murrelet* 34:41-46.

184 Ullrey, D. E., W. G. Vouatt, H. E. Johnson and L. D. Fry
1967 Protein requirements of white-tailed deer fawns. *Journal of Wildlife Management* 31(4):679-685.

Index

A

accidents, 35
acorns, 63-65, 98
Alaska, 76
alders, 27
alfalfa, 66, 67
Allen, Durward; 47
allowable forage crop, 29, 30
allowable use factor, 30-32
animal units, 32, 33
antler development, 48-50, 52
antlerless deer seasons, 100, 104, 105, 107
Appalachians, 28, 65
Arizona, 25, 42, 54, 58, 66
artificial feeding, 55, 60, 66-69
aspen, 59, 69, 94
Austria, 55

B

bacteria, 47
balsam, *see* fir
bark peeling, 55
bear as predator, 76
beech, 79
birch, 79
bitterbrush, 32, 40, 44, 53, 61-65, 81
bloat, 68
bobcat as predator, 76
British Columbia, 22, 42, 50, 51, 58, 99
browse lines, 24, 61
browse seed collection, 83, 84
browse seeding, 83-86
browseways, 89, 90
browsing tolerance, 30-34, 63
buck law, 47, 107
Bureau of Land Management, U.S.; 106
burning, controlled; 28, 87-89

C

calcium, 48
California, 14, 18, 20, 21, 24, 26, 32, 47, 51-54, 58, 62, 65, 90, 99
California, University of; 56, 64
Canada, 23, 76
carrying capacity, 17, 18, 21, 22, 33-35, 55, 102
cattle as competitors, 76-80
cedar, 22, 32, 38, 43, 53, 56, 69, 97
chaparral, 18, 53, 59, 79, 80-90
chemical brush killers, 89, 93
chokeberry, 44
Cleveland National Forest, 90
clovers, 59
Colorado, 41, 44, 67, 72, 77
Colorado Fish and Game Department, 69
commensals, 67, 68
competition with livestock, 32, 33
conifers, 22, 42
cooperative programs, 10, 22, 98, 106
cover, 13, 14, 18-24
coyote as predator, 75, 76

D

damage, deer; 55, 99-101
deer, European red; 12, 55, 79
deer-livestock relationships, 32, 33, 60, 76-80
density limits, 18, 24
density, population; 16, 18, 24
desert, 15
Devils Garden Deer Herd, 16, 32
digestion, 67, 68
diseases, 35, 47
Dixon, Joseph; 58, 64
dog, free-roaming, as predator, 76
dogwoods, 39, 69

E

eagle as predator, 76
edema, 68
Edwards Plateau, 15
elderberry, 69
essential oils, 41, 42
evolution, 11, 12, 74, 75, 102

F

farmland deer range, 101
fawn mortality, 26, 72, 73, 103
fawn production, 39, 45-48, 51, 55, 72
feeding mixtures, 66, 67
feeding, supplemental; 55, 60, 66-69
fertility, 47, 72, 73
fir, 22, 23, 42, 53, 66, 97, 99
fire, effects of; 23, 27, 28, 63, 79, 86, 87, 92, 93
food habits studies, 39-43, 76-80
food poisoning, 59
food requirements, 32-44, 77
food shortages, 34-36, 55
food values, 52, 53, 56-65
foot rot, 26
forage maintenance reserve, 29, 30
forage-population relationships, 16-18, 29-36
forbs, 57-61, 78, 82
Forest Service, U.S.; 98, 106
forestry, 10, 22-24, 79, 80, 91-101, 106

G

goats as competitors, 77
grasses, 30, 31, 57-61, 77-80, 86
grazing, 57-61, 77-80
greenbrier, 32
growth, 45, 46, 50, 51, 72

H

habitat management, 10, 22-24, 81-101, 106
hay, 26, 39, 66-68
hemlock, 43
herd units, 70-73
home range, 14-17
hunting, 55, 76, 104-106
hunting regulations, 47, 55, 104-105, 107
hunting zones, 70-83, 107

I

Idaho, 32, 72
inbreeding, 48

J

junipers, 41, 43

L

legumes, 59, 86
Leopold, Aldo; 18
lilacs, 32, 92
livestock-deer relationships, 32, 33, 66, 76-80
Louisiana, 99
lupine, 59

M

mahogony, birch-leaf; 89
mahogony, curl-leaf; 43
Maine, 21, 22, 97
management, deer; 34, 55, 69, 76, 86, 100, 102-107
manzanita, 92
maple, 31, 60, 69
Massachusetts, 43, 47, 48, 100
Michigan, 15, 53, 100
migratory deer, 14, 71, 72
minerals, 55, 59
Minnesota, 15, 94, 97
Minnesota Department of Conservation, 94
Minnesota Plan for Emergency Care of Deer, 69
Mississippi, 77
Missouri, 43, 58, 98
Missouri Department of Conservation, 98
Montana, 14
mortality, 11, 17, 26, 51, 52, 55, 59, 69, 72, 103
movements of deer, 14-17, 20, 21, 70-73, 99

N

Nevada, 15, 58
New England, 22, 43, 77
New Hampshire, 42, 55
New Mexico, 47
New York State, 25, 39, 43, 47, 66
New Zealand, 12, 79
North Carolina, 32
nutrition, effects of; 37-39, 45-55, 72, 73
nutritional requirements, 45-55, 66-69

O

oaks, 39, 44, 61-65, 79, 92
openings, 22, 23, 79, 86-90, 93-101
optimum density, 15, 16, 18
Oregon, 15, 51, 68
overbrowsing, 11, 17, 29, 41, 66-69, 72, 86
overgrazing, 27, 35, 78-80
overpopulations, 11, 12, 35, 36, 41, 48, 51, 57, 66-69, 72, 100, 103
Ozark Mountains, 43, 58

P

palatability of deer food, 37-44, 53
parasites, 51, 52, 55
penned deer experiments, 37-40, 42
Pennsylvania, 48, 52, 86, 100
phosphorus, 48
pines, 22, 38, 42, 61, 94
plant succession, 79
planting browse species, 83-87
poisonous plants, 39
population fluctuations, 35, 36
predation, 74-76
predator control, 67-68
pregnancy rates, 46-48, 51, 55, 72
protein deficiency, 52, 53
proteins, 42, 45, 48, 52-53, 59, 61, 69
pulpwood cutting, 96, 97

R

rabbitbrush, 41, 60
rabbits, 99
range management, 57, 59, 60, 78-80
redwood, 24
reproductive success, 46-48
restoration of deer, 9-10
rumen analysis, 39, 53

S

sagebrush, 40, 41, 53, 61-65, 79, 81
salt, 54, 68

sanctuaries, 100
Saskatchewan, 23
security factor, 19, 21
seed production, 29
serviceberry, 44
shade, 20
sheep as competitors, 76-80
Sierra Nevada, 14
snow, 26, 64, 75
soil conditions, 13, 39
South Dakota, 43, 58
spatial requirements, 18
spruces, 42, 97
starvation, 38, 42, 55, 67, 68
stocking, 10
stress, 51, 52, 54
sulphur, 54
sumac, 69
summer range, 15, 70-73

T

temperature, air; 20, 21, 25
Texas, 15, 33, 65, 77, 94
thiourea, 85
topography, 13
trace elements, 55
Trippensee, R. E.; 58

U

unit management, 70-73
Utah, 15, 41, 44, 51, 57-60, 67, 72, 77

V

Vancouver Island, 22
Vermont, 47
Virginia, 49, 106
Virginia Commission of Game and Inland Fisheries, 106

W

Washington, 23
water catchment devices, 28
water requirements, 25, 26
water supplies, 13, 18, 25-28
Western Association of State Fish and Game Commissioners, 83
willows, 27, 69
winter die-offs, 17, 47, 53, 55, 68, 69, 72, 103
winter range, 15, 20, 22, 51, 57, 70-73, 78, 97
winter survival, 51, 55, 72
Wisconsin, 15, 37, 66, 76, 86, 94, 100
Wisconsin Agricultural Research Experiment Station, 54
wolf, 75, 76

Y

yards, 15, 20, 22, 51, 57, 70-73, 93-101
yaupon, 94
yew, 43